MW00898957

YOUNG STUDENTS

Learning Library

VOLUME 22

World War II–Index

WEEKLY READER BOOKS

MIDDLETOWN·CONNECTICUT

PHOTO CREDITS

Young Students Learning Library is a trademark of Field Publications.

ISBN 0-8374-6052-2

CONTENTS

WORLD WAR II The Great War (World War I) was called "the war to end all wars." When it ended in 1919, people generally believed that nothing so terrible could happen again. But within 20 years, nations around the globe were plunged into another world war that lasted from September 1, 1939, to September 2, 1945, and in which more than 50 million people lost their lives.

As in World War I, the opposing armies of World War II were made up of two groups of nations. The *Axis Powers* included Germany, Italy, and Japan. The *Allied Powers* included Great Britain and other members of the Commonwealth of Nations, the United States, the Soviet Union, France, and China.

The areas of major fighting were in Europe, northern Africa, Asia, and in the Pacific, Atlantic, and Indian oceans. Battles took place on land, sea, and in the air with a power and destructiveness never before experienced in history. Nuclear bombs were developed and used for the first time, as were high-altitude, supersonic rocket missiles and jet planes.

Events Leading to War At the end of World War I, Europe was in a shambles. The Treaty of Versailles had exacted harsh repayment from Germany, which that country was unable to provide. The United States did not join the League of Nations, preferring to stay out of European affairs. Nations became concerned with their own internal problems. Members of the League of Nations were not enthusiastic about enforcing international agreements made by the League.

In the early 1930's, a great economic depression hit the United

◀ *U.S. Marines in action against the Japanese in the Pacific during World War II. A news cameraman crouches in the foreground.*

States and Europe. In Germany, as in other countries, prices increased as wages and jobs decreased. The government leadership that had developed in Germany after World War I was unable to cope with the economic conditions. Into this situation stepped Adolf Hitler, head of the Nazi (National Socialist) Party. On January 30, 1933, Hitler became Chancellor of Germany. He promised to make Germany the strongest nation on earth and began increasing production of military supplies. Other countries recognized that Hitler was gaining power, but few people believed he would actually go to war.

Europe was having political as well as economic troubles in the 1920's and 1930's. After World War I, the empire of Austria-Hungary had been broken up into a group of smaller nations—Yugoslavia, Albania, Hungary, Czechoslovakia, and Austria—that were all suspicious of each other. The Soviet Union had gained in industrial and military strength, and most Western powers were fearful of Stalin's dictatorial regime. In 1922, Benito Mussolini came to power as dictator of Italy and set out to build up the Italian military forces. For defense, France fortified the Maginot Line, a series of forts and huge concrete bunkers along their border with Germany. But the Maginot fortifications did not extend along France's Belgian border, where German forces had first invaded France in World War I.

In 1931, Japan attacked China. When the League of Nations ordered Japan to withdraw from China, Japan ignored the order and resigned from the League in 1933. Hitler, noting that the League was powerless to stop Japan's aggression, decided to take over former German lands along the Rhine River. In 1936, Hitler's troops moved into the Rhineland unopposed. In the same year, Mussolini's troops conquered Ethiopia and forced the emperor, Haile Selassie, into ex-

▲ *Germany's leader, Adolf Hitler (right), meets with Britain's peace-seeking prime minister, Neville Chamberlain, in 1938.*

The Allied invasion of France on June 6, 1944, was the greatest naval invasion the world has ever seen. Over 150,000 soldiers from the U.S. and British armies stormed ashore on five beaches. They were supported by about 12,000 airplanes, 350 warships, and 6,100 landing craft.

During World War II, between 55 and 60 million people were killed, the greatest loss of life in any war. Over a third of this number were Russians. About 10 million people had been killed in World War I.

WORLD WAR II FIGHTERS

▲ *The German Focke-Wulf FW190. Top speed: 410 miles per hour (660 km/h).*

▲ *The American Mustang P-51. Top speed: 435 miles per hour (700 km/h).*

▲ *The American Republic P-47 Thunderbolt. Top speed: 430 miles per hour (690 km/h).*

▲ *The Russian Mikoyan MiG-3. Top speed: 405 miles per hour (650 km/h).*

▲ *The Japanese Nakajima Ki-84. Top speed: 380 miles per hour (610 km/h).*

ile. Throughout 1936 and 1937, Germany and Italy gave military support to Generalissimo Francisco Franco in the Spanish civil war. In 1938, Hitler took over Austria without a battle. He then demanded the Sudetenland, the borderlands of Czechoslovakia. France, Czechoslovakia's main ally, and Britain gave the borderlands to Hitler through negotiations resulting in the Munich Pact of 1938. In March 1939, Hitler moved in and seized all of Czechoslovakia.

Europe was slow to realize Hitler's plan for world domination in spite of his speeches declaring the Germans to be superior to all other people. Most governments felt that Hitler was a reasonable man and could be dealt with by negotiation and *appeasement* (giving in to Hitler's demands in order to maintain peace). But appeasement was not working.

The Fighting EUROPE FROM 1939–1942. On August 23, 1939, Hitler and Joseph Stalin (premier of the Soviet Union) signed a pact agreeing not to attack each other. They also agreed to invade and divide Poland. Great Britain and France warned that if Poland were attacked, they would declare war on Germany. But Hitler knew that neither France nor Britain could seriously attack Germany without help from the Soviet Union. On September 1, 1939, German forces crashed through Poland. On September 3, Britain and France, joined by countries of the Commonwealth of Nations, declared war on Germany. German *blitzkrieg* ("lightning warfare") tactics—a combination of tanks and motor artillery with air support (bombs)—were overwhelming. The Soviet Union attacked from the east, and after one month Poland fell.

Among Hitler's troops was a special S.S. corps. "S.S." stood for *Schutzstaffel*, meaning "protection staff" or "defense corps." The S.S. troops were first organized in the 1920's as Hitler's personal body-

guards. But the corps had since grown to tremendous strength and was under the direction of Heinrich Himmler, Hitler's police chief. The S.S. corps took over and ran a country once it was conquered. In Poland, as in other countries, the S.S. deliberately set out to kill all Jews (whom Hitler blamed for Germany's troubles) and to kill all people capable of leadership.

After Poland, the Soviet Union conquered part of Finland. The German army attacked and occupied Norway and Denmark. The British prime minister, Neville Chamberlain, was forced to resign because of his ineffective policies against Germany.

Winston Churchill was made prime minister on May 10, 1940—the day Germany invaded Belgium and the Netherlands. The confident Germans swept southward into France, as they had in World War I, avoiding the Maginot Line that the French army had been so long preparing. The British tried to help France, but were forced northward to the port of Dunkirk on the English Channel, from which they withdrew back to England. On May 28, King Leopold III of Belgium surrendered to the Germans. The French tried to defend Paris, but the capital was taken on June 14. The French government

▼ *During the air war, Allied bombers, such as these British Stirlings, attacked targets in Germany.*

▲ *U.S. troops man an anti-tank gun positioned to command a beach.*

bomb the city of London. But this was a mistake because it gave the British air force a chance to repair damaged planes and fit out new aircraft. British planes beat off the German air force, and the Battle of Britain was broken off by the Germans in the autumn of 1940.

Hitler sent a strong army and tank force under General Erwin Rommel into Africa on February 12, 1941. British and Commonwealth troops were forced to spend two years fighting Rommel's Afrika Korps, which kept many Allied troops from defending Asia against Japan.

On October 28, 1940, without telling Hitler, Mussolini sprang a surprise attack on Greece. This attack brought in the British to defend Greece. The British attacked the Italian fleet at Taranto, Italy, and fought Italian troops in Greece. Hitler was furious. British troops were now close to the Romanian oil fields that Hitler planned to use as the fuel supply for Germany's invasion of the Soviet Union. Hitler had to get the British out of Greece, but the Yugoslav government refused to provide the needed railroad transport for Hitler's troops. Hitler decided to utterly destroy Yugoslavia. This meant he had to delay his invasion of the Soviet Union from May 15 until June 22, 1941. This delay was a terrible mistake. The invasion brought the Soviet Union to the Allied Powers' side.

The Germans attacked the Soviet Union along three fronts. But Hitler had delayed the invasion too long, and the terrible Russian winter set in. He had also gravely underestimated the strength of Soviet forces. After months of bitter fighting, especially in Stalingrad (now Volgograd), the German forces had run out of supplies and willpower. They were forced to retreat, and the Soviets began their push toward Germany in 1943.

THE PACIFIC FROM 1940–1942. The fighting in Europe had left many Asian nations with inadequate de-

▲ *Allied military leaders: General Eisenhower (left), supreme commander of Allied forces in Europe, and General Montgomery.*

signed an armistice with Gemany on June 22. The whole northern half of France was now in German hands. The southern half was headed by Marshal Henri Petain with headquarters at the town of Vichy. This Vichy Government, because of its armistice with Hitler, was repudiated by many French people who called themselves the "Free French." The Free French determined to use any means to free France from German domination.

The Germans had built up a powerful *Luftwaffe* (air force), and Marshal Hermann Goering, the Luftwaffe chief, set out to conquer Britain by air. However, the British had also developed a strong air force and an extensive radar warning system. On July 10, the Luftwaffe began bombing British airfields, ports, bridges, factories, and power plants. Later, Goering ordered the Luftwaffe to

After the Battle of Britain, Prime Minister Churchill paid a famous tribute to the courageous young pilots of the Royal Air Force. His words were: "Never in the field of human conflict has so much been owed by so many to so few."

ОТСТОИМ
ВОЛГУ-МАТУШ[

▲ *This Soviet poster proclaims: "We will defend Mother Volga." The Soviet troops prevented the German invaders from crossing the Volga River.*

▼ *The Battle of Britain in 1940 was a crucial struggle. The British victory prevented a German invasion of the British Isles. Among the most famous warplanes was the British Spitfire fighter, shown here.*

◄ *On D-Day, June 6, 1944, the Allies began the liberation of Western Europe. In the first week after the seaborne landing, they poured more than 325,000 troops into northern France.*

MAJOR EVENTS OF WORLD WAR II

Sept. 1939	Germany invades Poland; signs non-aggression pact with Soviet Union. Britain and France declare war on Germany.
April/May 1940	German troops conquer most of Western Europe.
July/Sept. 1940	Battle of Britain.
Oct. 1940	Italy joins war on German side. Axis forces overrun Balkans and North Africa.
June 1941	Germany invades Soviet Union.
Dec. 1941	Pearl Harbor attack. U.S. declares war on Axis powers.
Jan./March 1942	Japanese capture Philippines, Java, Burma.
May/June 1942	U.S. and Japanese fleets in naval battles of Coral Sea and Midway.
July 1942	Battle of El Alamein; British halt Axis advance in North Africa.
Nov. 1942	Allies land in west North Africa.
Feb. 1943	Germans surrender at Stalingrad.
July/Sept. 1943	Allies invade Italy; Italy signs armistice.
June 1944	D-Day landings by Allied armies in France.
Dec. 1944	Battle of the Bulge, last German attack in Western Europe.
Feb. 1945	U.S. forces liberate Philippines; battle for Iwo Jima. Allied leaders meet at Yalta.
April 1945	German leader Hitler commits suicide as Berlin falls to Soviet armies.
May 7, 1945	Germany surrenders.
June 1945	U.S. forces fight for Okinawa, Japan.
Aug. 1945	Atomic bombs dropped on Hiroshima and Nagasaki.
Sept. 2, 1945	Japan surrenders.

SECOND WORLD WAR IN EUROPE

SECOND WORLD WAR IN THE PACIFIC

▶ *U.S. airplanes sink the Japanese aircraft carrier* Shoho *at the Battle of Coral Sea, May 1942 (taken from a painting by Robert Benny).*

The Battle of Leyte Gulf in the Philippines, in October 1944, involved the highest number of ships and aircraft ever to fight in a single air and sea battle. More than 150 U.S. and allied ships took part against Japanese ships, and over 1,200 U.S. aircraft flew in the battle.

▲ *German defeat at Stalingrad. In tattered uniforms, German soldiers march in the bitter cold as they are taken prisoner by the Soviet forces.*

fenses. Japan hungered after the oil and iron ore that were available in other Asian countries. In September 1940, Japan signed a military pact with the Axis powers and immediately took over part of French Indochina (now Vietnam). From there, Japan planned to take the Dutch East Indies, the Philippines, Malaya, Thailand, Burma, and various islands in the Pacific Ocean.

The United States, however, had moved its Pacific fleet closer to Japan—to a base at Pearl Harbor, Hawaii. The U.S. fleet was the only real threat to Japan. Japanese Admiral Isoroku Yamamoto insisted that a war with the United States had to begin with the bombing of Pearl Harbor. Early on December 7, 1941, Japanese planes roared over the Pearl Harbor base. The attack was a complete surprise to the United States, but it failed to destroy the entire U.S. fleet, the repair yards, or the fuel depots. On December 8, President Franklin Roosevelt asked Congress to declare war on Japan. Three days later, Germany and Italy declared war on the United States in support of Japan. Admiral Chester W. Nimitz took command of U.S. naval operations in the Pacific. General Douglas MacArthur became the Pacific army commander.

By the spring of 1942, Japanese forces had conquered most of southeast Asia, the Dutch East Indies, and the Philippines. But the United States was mobilizing quickly. U.S. factories churned out guns, aircraft, tanks, ships, and other supplies for use against the Germans in Europe and the Japanese in the Pacific. The Japanese planned to establish a line of military bases extending from the Aleutian Islands (off the tip of Alaska) across the central Pacific through Wake Island and the Marshall Islands, then westward to New Guinea and Burma. Except for the Aleutian bases, this Japanese defense system was set by May 1942. The Japanese

▲ *The Germans fighting in the snow outside Moscow. The soldiers are dressed in white to act as camouflage against the snow.*

then decided to take Midway Island and Australia.

Early in 1942, the United States broke the Japanese military communications code. From then on, the United States knew Japanese plans in advance. In the Battle of the Coral Sea from May 5 to 8, U.S. ships kept Japan from threatening Australia. Admiral Nimitz next learned of Japan's plan to take Midway Island. In the Battle of Midway from June 3 to 6, the United States destroyed Japan's air superiority in the Pacific.

ALLIED COOPERATION. After U.S. entry into the war, the British and U.S. forces decided to combine their efforts. President Roosevelt and Prime Minister Churchill set up the Anglo-American Combined Chiefs of Staff (CCS) with headquarters in Washington, D.C. The British chief was Field Marshal Sir John Dill; the U.S. chief was General George C. Marshall. The CCS kept contact with Stalin's military advisory group.

In 1942, the Soviet Union was taking the brunt of Hitler's war effort. The CCS promised to aid the Soviets with supplies. They also decided that an Allied invasion force was needed to break into Europe from the Atlantic coast and drive the Germans eastward. In May 1942, the British started a policy of "saturation bombing." Heavy bombing raids were now started on German industrial cities, disrupting supplies of arms to the Soviet and African fronts.

The Allies invaded North Africa in November 1942. British Field Marshal Bernard Montgomery and U.S. General George S. Patton forced the surrender of the German Africa Korps on May 14, 1943. Montgomery and Patton then invaded the Italian island of Sicily, which was to be used as an Allied air base. On July 25, Italy's King Victor Emmanuel III dismissed Mussolini as prime minister. Hitler sent troops into Italy to fight the invading Allies, but on October 13, the Italian government joined the Allies and declared war on Germany.

In the Pacific, the U.S. Navy was the Allies' only large force to push the Japanese off the many islands they had captured. By June 1943, General Douglas MacArthur had driven the Japanese from New Guinea. U.S. troops soundly defeated a large Japanese force at the Battle of Guadalcanal.

In December 1943, General Dwight D. Eisenhower was appointed to command an Allied invasion of Europe. The first landings would be made on the beaches of Normandy in northern France. At

this location, troops could move inland quickly, and air bases in Britain could provide continuous fighter cover. The Pas de Calais, across the English Channel from Dover, was the only other location to fit these characteristics. Eisenhower bluffed the Germans into thinking that the main invasion would take place from Dover and that the Normandy landing farther west would be a fake.

On D-Day (June 6, 1944) the first wave of Allied troops hit the beaches at Normandy under a tremendous cover of naval and air bombardment. Allied aircraft destroyed bridges, railways, and roads leading to Normandy in order to delay the arrival of German reinforcements. The remaining Allied invasion force landed, using artificial harbors towed across from England, and began pushing the Germans out of France, Belgium, and the Netherlands. Germany now had to fight on three fronts—in Italy, in the Soviet Union, and in France. Fast-moving tank forces led by General George Patton encircled and demolished German army groups in France. A Free French division under General Charles de Gaulle moved southward and liberated Paris on August 24. Armies under the command of General Omar Bradley continued to push the Germans back toward the Rhine River.

Meanwhile, Soviet troops were de-

▲ *Cities suffered terrible destruction from air raids. Here, the walls of a bombed building tumble near St. Paul's Cathedral in London during a German air raid on the city. The cathedral itself survived.*

◄ *German U-boats (submarines) preyed on Allied convoys. The escorting warships hunted the U-boats with sonar and depth charges. This painting shows a surfaced U-boat being attacked by an Allied destroyer.*

▲ *U.S. Marines plant the United States flag at the summit of Mount Suribachi on the Pacific island of Iwo Jima, February 23, 1943. A famous picture captured by Joe Rosenthal.*

▼ *Crowds of Parisians, celebrating the liberation of their city by the Allied armies, scatter for cover as a sniper fires from a building on the Place de la Concorde.*

molishing German forces in their move westward through what is now Poland, East Germany, Czechoslovakia, Hungary, Romania, Bulgaria, and Yugoslavia. On June 13, 1944, Hitler began launching V-1 and V-2 missiles—rocket-powered warheads aimed at London. They killed and wounded thousands of British citizens but did not halt the progress of the war.

On September 11, Allied troops crossed the western border of Germany. Germany was being squeezed from all sides, but Hitler had no intention of giving up. He speeded up production of war supplies and especially of his new jet airplanes.

On December 16, Hitler launched a great counterattack on the Allies in the west by taking soldiers and equipment away from the eastern front. At first, Germany was successful in pushing the Allies back—creating a bulge in the Allied line. Hitler's forces fought bitterly to keep their advantage in this Battle of the Bulge. But German losses were so high that they were forced to retreat on January 8, 1945. During March and April, Allied forces took the great German industrial area in the Ruhr Valley. On April 25, U.S. and Soviet patrols met

▲ *The B-17 Flying Fortress was the mainstay of U.S. Army Air Force daylight bombing raids in Europe.*

along the Elbe River. This was the eastern limit of the U.S. advance—75 miles (120 km) short of Berlin—that had been agreed upon between the Soviet Union and the Western Allies. U.S. forces under General Patton crossed to the southeast to take Austria. Germany was completely overrun.

On April 30, 1945, Adolf Hitler committed suicide at his underground headquarters in Berlin. Surrender terms were signed with Germany on May 7, and the war in Europe was officially over on May 8 (V-E Day). Hitler's attempt at world domination had failed, Germany was in ruins, and the German people were prisoners of war in their own country.

VICTORY IN THE PACIFIC. In 1943, the U.S. Pacific command was joined by British Admiral Lord Louis Mountbatten. He directed successful maneuvers to drive the Japanese from Burma, Malaya, the Dutch East Indies, Thailand, and French Indochina. Admiral Nimitz planned to capture certain Pacific islands to be used as bases for attacks on the Japanese home islands. One after another, U.S. forces took Tarawa (now part of Kiribati), Kwajalein (the main island of Japanese defense in the Marshall Islands), and Saipan, Tinian, Rota, and Guam (all part of the Mariana Islands).

Meanwhile, Japanese Admiral Jisaburo Ozawa steamed toward the Philippine Sea with orders to destroy the U.S. fleet stationed there. The Battle of the Philippine Sea, on June 19, 1944, was the greatest carrier battle of the war. The Japanese were left with almost nothing. U.S. forces eventually took the Philippines early in 1945. During that operation, severe damage was done by Japanese *kamikaze* pilots—suicide pilots who attacked by sending their planes loaded with bombs directly at a target and blowing themselves up.

On November 24, 1944, U.S. planes based in the Marianas began bombing Tokyo and other Japanese home targets. However, the flying distance was too great. Damaged U.S. planes could not make the long trip back to base. To get closer to Japan, the United States attacked and took the island of Iwo Jima after fierce fighting that lasted from February 19 to March 16, 1945. U.S. bomber attacks from Iwo Jima did tremendous damage to Japanese industry, but the Japanese would not surrender unless their home islands were invaded. U.S. troops began preparing for this invasion by capturing the island of Okinawa on May 31.

Early in August, President Harry S. Truman ordered the use of atomic weapons against Japan. The first atomic bomb ever used in warfare was exploded over the city of Hiroshima on August 6, 1945. The second atomic bomb was exploded over Nagasaki on August 9. On the same day, the Soviet Union declared war on Japan and captured Manchuria. On August 14, 1945, Japanese Emperor Hirohito accepted Allied surrender terms. The surrender became official on September 2 (V-J Day), and World War II was finally ended.

The Terms of Peace As a result of agreements made during the war, Germany was to be demilitarized and occupied by two powers. The Soviets occupied East Germany, which has

since become the German Democratic Republic. The Allies occupied West Germany, which has since become the Federal Republic of Germany. The city of Berlin was split into four sectors, or zones—one each for the Soviet Union, Great Britain, France, and the United States. The former Soviet zone is now East Berlin, the capital of the German Democratic Republic. The other Allied zones were combined, forming the city of West Berlin, which belongs to the Federal Republic of Germany.

Japan was demilitarized and occupied by U.S. troops until 1952. The United States initiated the Marshall Plan, whereby it lent huge sums of money and material to war-torn countries to help them rebuild. The Soviet Union took control in the countries it occupied, and the Communist governments based on the Soviet system were established in Hungary, Czechoslovakia, Bulgaria, Yugoslavia, Poland, and Romania.

On October 24, 1945, the United Nations was established to help ensure peace.

ALSO READ: AIRCRAFT CARRIER; ARMY; CHURCHILL, WINSTON; DE GAULLE, CHARLES; EISENHOWER, DWIGHT D.; HITLER, ADOLF; INTERNATIONAL RELATIONS; MACARTHUR, DOUGLAS; MARINE CORPS; MISSILE; MUSSOLINI, BENITO; NAVY; NUCLEAR ENERGY; PEARL HARBOR; ROOSEVELT, FRANKLIN D.;

▲ *Allied leaders met at Yalta, in the Soviet Union, in 1945. From left to right: Churchill, Roosevelt, and Stalin.*

▼ *The end of the war in Europe, May 7, 1945. Cheering crowds throng the streets of London; among them are U.S. soldiers.*

▲ *The U.S. forces bore the brunt of the Pacific war against the Japanese. To bring about Japan's surrender, President Truman ordered the dropping of atomic bombs on the cities of Hiroshima and Nagasaki. The huge mushroom-shaped cloud of the second explosion, marking the destruction of Nagasaki, heralded the end of the war in the Pacific.*

The soil is full of earthworms. There are so many of them that if all the worms in the soil of the United States were weighed, they would be ten times as heavy as the whole human population.

The largest worm is the Giant Gippsland earthworm of Victoria, Australia. It can be 12 feet (3.7 m) long and ¾ inch (2 cm) thick.

STALIN, JOSEPH; SUBMARINE; TANK; TITO; TREATY; TRUMAN, HARRY S.; UNITED NATIONS; WAR; WORLD WAR I. *See article at name of each country involved.*

WORM Worms are slender animals with soft bodies and no backbones. They vary greatly in their sizes, shapes, and habitats. Some worms, like the common earthworm, are familiar to everyone. Other worms, such as those that live deep in the ocean, are seldom seen. Some worms are so small that they can only be seen under a microscope. All kinds of worms need plenty of moisture to survive. In fact, most of them are water dwellers.

Roundworms, or *nematodes*, live almost anywhere in enormous numbers. They are tiny, thin worms that look something like fine bits of thread. Many roundworms are *parasites*, or animals that must live on, or inside, some other kind of animal or plant. Hookworms and pinworms live in the bodies of mammals, including human beings. Roundworms that are plant parasites inhabit the roots of plants and cause millions of dollars' worth of damage each year to farmers.

Flatworms receive their name from their flattened bodies. Some are less than half an inch (13 mm) long. Tapeworms, which are a kind of flatworm, may grow to be 50 feet (15 m) long in the intestines of large animals. All tapeworms are parasites. Flukes are flatworms that may live in the blood, liver, or other body parts of animals. Some flukes cause serious illness to human beings in Africa and Asia. Planaria are freshwater flatworms. They swim about in lakes and ponds, scavenging for food.

The very long ribbon worms are not parasites. Most ribbon worms live in the ocean. You can find different kinds of ribbon worms under rocks near the seashore. One, the sand-

worm, is often used as fishing bait.

The common earthworm is in the big group of worms called *annelida*, or segmented worms. Annelids are not related to other kinds of worms. The bodies of annelids are divided into sections, or segments. Many annelids live in the ocean. Bloodworms are annelids that live in shallow parts of the ocean. They have bright red bodies. At one end of its body, the bloodworm has a *proboscis*, which looks like a small tube. The proboscis shoots out quickly, attaches itself to food, and then is drawn back into the body.

Clam worms are also common ocean dwellers. Clam worms have

▼ *The fanworm is a marine bristleworm. It uses its feathery tentacles to trap tiny particles of food. It lives inside a protective tube.*

Common earthworm

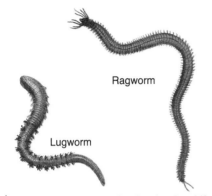

Ragworm

Lugworm

▲ *The earthworm is a land animal, while lugworms and ragworms live on the seabed and shore.*

tiny paddles on each segment of their body. They are active swimmers. They can also burrow in sand and mud. During the breeding season, clam worms swarm in large numbers near the water's surface to mate. Some sea worms are not active swimmers. They spend most of their time in tunnels or burrows. The parchment worm lives in a tunnel in the mud. The tunnel provides a protective covering for the parchment worm's fragile body. Other sea worms build tubes or tunnels with hard, limey material. The *serpula* often covers rocks and seashells with its whitish tunnels.

ALSO READ: ANIMAL KINGDOM, EARTH-WORM, PARASITE.

WRESTLING The sport of wrestling is one of the oldest in the world. The art of almost all ancient civilizations showed scenes of people wrestling. There are Egyptian wall paintings over 5,000 years old and ancient Japanese sculptures that show wrestlers in action. The sport was included in the first Olympic Games, which were held by the Greeks in 776 B.C.

Wrestling is basically a test of strength, quickness, and stamina (endurance). A good wrestler must also know how to use a variety of *holds*. A hold is a grip you apply to your opponent's body that makes it difficult for him or her to use any strength and helps you to throw your opponent to the ground. All wrestling matches are fought on a padded canvas mat. There are two main styles of the sport. The first is the *freestyle*, or *catch-as-catch-can*, style which is common in the United States. The *Greco-Roman* style is popular in Europe. Both styles are contested in the Olympic Games. In freestyle wrestling, contestants are allowed to apply holds below the waist of their opponents and to trip and tackle them. In the Greco-Roman style, wrestlers cannot trip or tackle, they cannot apply holds to their opponents' legs, and they cannot use their own legs to grip or squeeze their opponents.

In both styles, wrestlers compete in their own weight classes since it would be unfair for one person to wrestle with a much heavier opponent. The winner of a match either pins the opponent's shoulders to the mat, or scores more points than the opponent. Points are scored for falls, for applying holds, and for ability and aggressiveness. College wrestling matches are divided into three periods of three minutes each. High school matches are divided into three two-

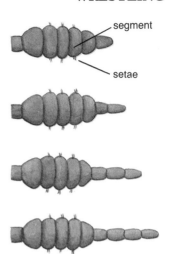

segment

setae

▲ *Each segment of an earthworm's body has four pairs of small bristles, called setae. These bristles dig into the soil as the earthworm burrows. An earthworm moves by contracting (shortening) and lengthening its segments, in a series of wavelike ripples.*

▼ *Sumo wrestlers take guard in a Tokyo wrestling hall. Whichever wrestler is forced out of the ring or down on the floor is the loser.*

minute periods. In all amateur matches, the contestants are not allowed to use punishing holds, such as a headlock, strangle hold, or a scissors. The scissors hold is one in which the legs are used like a pair of scissors to squeeze any part of an opponent's body.

Professional wrestling used to be much like the amateur sport, but in recent years, it has become a fake exhibition of brutality. Professional wrestlers entertain the spectators by seeming to slug, bounce, and kick each other around. Actually professional wrestling is a well-rehearsed act. It looks savage but the contestants do little harm to each other.

One of the most popular sports in Japan is *sumo* wrestling. Sumo contestants weigh about 300 pounds (136 kg) and have great strength. The matches are held in a large circle and the winner is the one who makes any part of the opponent's body, other than the feet, touch the ground. Sumo champions are national heroes in Japan.

ALSO READ: SPORTS.

▲ *Amateur wrestlers attempt to topple over each other. This style of wrestling is often called the Greco-Roman style, referring to the ancient Olympic games where it was the most popular sport.*

▲ *Frank Lloyd Wright, U.S. architect.*

WRIGHT, FRANK LLOYD
(1867–1959) Frank Lloyd Wright was one of the most influential architects of modern times. He was born in Richland Center, Wisconsin. He studied under the American architect, Louis Sullivan. Wright set up his own office in Chicago in 1893. Most new buildings at that time were decorated with classical (Greek and Roman) arches and columns. But Wright began to design buildings with simple, bold lines and no fussy decoration. One of his main aims was to give as much freedom and space as possible to the people living or working inside. His "prairie" houses have rooms that open into one another with very few dividing walls. Wright believed that a house should blend with its surrounding landscape. He

▲ *Falling Water, built in Pennsylvania in 1936, was Frank Lloyd Wright's ultimate private house—blending nature and man-made materials into organic architecture.*

called this idea "organic architecture." One of Wright's most spectacular buildings is the Solomon R. Guggenheim Museum in New York City. The galleries are arranged around a huge spiral ramp.

Wright founded the Taliesin Fellowship, a community and school for young architects. The community is now centered at Wright's winter home, Taliesin West, near Scottsdale, Arizona.

ALSO READ: ARCHITECTURE.

WRIGHT, RICHARD (1908–1960)
Richard Wright was one of America's most important black writers. He was born near Natchez, Mississippi. His mother was crippled and unable to take care of him for most of his childhood, so he had to live in orphanages or with poor relatives.

Wright went to Chicago, Illinois, in the 1930's, and worked at many jobs while beginning his career as a writer. He joined the Federal Writers Project, a government agency created to help writers during the economic depression of the 1930's. For a while, Wright believed that the Communist party could offer hope to black Americans, but he later decided that the movement did not live up to its ideals.

Wright's first published work was a collection of four stories, *Uncle Tom's Children,* about racial prejudice in the South. His best-known book, *Native Son,* tells how the pressure of trying to survive in the slums of Chicago drives a young black man to commit murder. In *Black Boy,* which is based on his own unhappy childhood, Wright describes the terrible effects of poverty and racial hatred on a growing child.

Other books by Wright include *Twelve Million Black Voices; The Outsider; Black Power; White Man, Listen!;* and *The Long Dream.* Wright's work is a bitter, unforgiving description of the miseries, discouragement, and hatred brought about by racial prejudice in the United States. Wright left the United States in 1950 and lived in Paris, France, for the rest of his life.

ALSO READ: BLACK AMERICANS, LITERATURE.

WRIGHT BROTHERS Wilbur Wright (1867–1912) and Orville Wright (1871–1948) were U.S. inventors and aviators. They built and piloted the world's first successful power-driven airplane.

Wilbur was born near New Castle, Indiana, and Orville was born in Dayton, Ohio. In 1892, they opened a bicycle repair shop and later designed and manufactured bicycles. They became interested in a type of unpowered airplane, called a *glider,* which was being built in Europe. The brothers taught themselves *aeronautics* (the science of flight) and built their own glider. They made their first glider flight in 1900 at Kitty Hawk, North Carolina. Their glider was a biplane,

with two wings, one above the other. The brothers built two other biplane gliders that they flew at Kill Devil Hill near Kitty Hawk in 1901 and 1902. One glider made a record flight of more than 600 feet (182 m). The brothers also built a wind tunnel to experiment with different air pressures on the wings of their gliders.

In the winter of 1902, they designed a propeller powered by a lightweight gasoline engine, which was fitted onto a large biplane that they named "Flyer I." At Kill Devil Hill on December 17, 1903, Orville Wright piloted the first powered flight. Later that day, Wilbur made a flight of 852 feet (260 m).

The brothers continued to improve their airplane design and built several more biplanes. During 1908, Wilbur gave flying demonstrations in Europe. On one flight, he stayed in the air for 2 hours and 20 minutes. The brothers opened their own airplane company in New York City in 1909.

After Wilbur died of typhoid, Orville continued to design and manufacture airplanes. The site of the Wright brothers' first flight at Kitty Hawk is now preserved as the Wright Brothers National Monument.

ALSO READ: AIRPLANE, AVIATION, GLIDER.

▲ *Richard Wright, U.S. writer.*

▲ *Wilbur (left) and Orville Wright.*

▼ *Orville Wright piloting the "Baby Wright."*

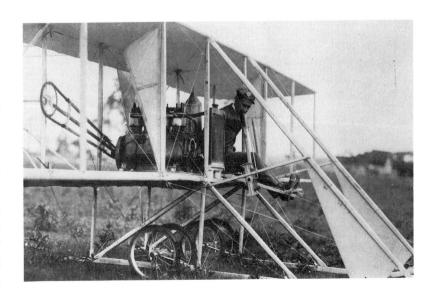

▲ *One of the earliest forms of writing was Egyptian hieroglyphics. Figures or objects were used to represent words or sounds. This example of hieroglyphics is from the wall of an Egyptian pharoah's tomb.*

▲ *The Maya Indians of Central America erected this stone pillar, or stele, about 1,000 years ago in Copan, Honduras. It is covered with carved hieroglyphics.*

WRITTEN LANGUAGE When you speak, you make certain sounds in order to communicate with other people. The speech sounds you make are *word symbols*. A word symbol always stands for, or represents, something. For example, when someone says "dog," you immediately think of a certain type of animal. When someone says "hello," you know this is a greeting. When someone says "happy," you think of a certain type of feeling. If someone said "sobaka," it wouldn't mean anything to you because that word symbol is not part of your language. Languages are simply various systems of spoken word symbols.

Most day-to-day communication among people is done in spoken language—by talking. But much communication is also done in written language—by writing. When people write, they make certain marks on paper or some other material. The written marks are symbols standing for the words of spoken language.

Written language was not invented by any one person at any particular time or place. Writing evolved gradually as people needed ways to keep lasting records. By writing things down, people could communicate in a way more permanent and lasting than speech. Spoken language is not permanent. Once you have said something, that particular communication ends and cannot be heard again unless you keep repeating it over and over.

Drawings on the walls of caves were probably the earliest attempts by human beings to express themselves in writing. The cave paintings were not actually writing as we know it. But like writing, they were created by people in order to express something they had seen or thought about. Pictures eventually became used as written word symbols. In early picture writing, each picture stood for the object it represented. A picture of a sun stood for the sun. A picture of a sheep stood for a sheep.

Additional meanings were gradually assigned to the picture signs. A picture of the sun, for example, might stand for "day," "light," or "warmth." A sheep might stand for "wool" or just "animal." A house might stand for "shelter," "home," "building," or a number of other ideas. Each picture symbol stood for a whole word.

Another important development in written language was the *syllabary*. Syllabaries are writing systems in which syllables, rather than whole words, are represented each by a separate symbol. The Japanese writing system uses a syllabary.

The type of writing used in most Western languages is the alphabetic system. It was developed by the ancient Greeks from earlier symbols used by the Phoenicians. The Greeks assigned one symbol (letter) for each spoken sound. The alphabet you use for writing is made up of 26 symbols that stand for various speech sounds. The symbols B-A-R-N, written in that order, represent four speech sounds that together make up a spoken word. The spoken word, in turn, is a symbol standing for a real barn— a building where farm animals are kept. There are various alphabets in use—Roman, Greek, Hebrew, Ara-

▼ *This beautifully decorated page is from a book that was handwritten in Latin in 1156.*

bic, Cyrillic, Devanagari—but all are based on the idea of letters standing for speech sounds.

ALSO READ: ALPHABET, BRAILLE, COMMUNICATION, CROSSWORD PUZZLE, DICTIONARY, GRAMMAR, HANDWRITING, HIEROGLYPHICS, LANGUAGE ARTS, LANGUAGES, LITERACY, PRINTING, SHORTHAND, SPEECH, SPELLING, WORD GAMES.

WYOMING A visitor to a dude ranch in Wyoming can ride horses over mountain trails, go camping and fishing, and perhaps take a boat ride on a river. In the capital city of Cheyenne during the Frontier Days festival in July, a visitor can see Indian dances and rodeo events, with cowboys and cowgirls riding bucking broncos and wrestling steers. Wyoming is one of the largest states in size and the smallest in population.

The Land and Climate Wyoming belongs to the group of Rocky Mountain States. Other mountain states are north, west, and south of it. Montana is to the north and northwest, and Idaho is to the west. Southwest is Utah, and Colorado is to the south. On the east are South Dakota and Nebraska.

Wide basins lie between the tall ranges of the Rocky Mountains. The Big Horn Basin is in the north central part of the state. The Wyoming Basin is in the south central region. Large river systems start from the Continental Divide in Wyoming. The Snake River flows west to join the Columbia, and the Green River flows south into the Colorado.

In eastern Wyoming, the Great Plains slope toward the east. They are hilly, and they are cut by many rivers. The plains are lower than the mountains, but even so, they are high. The lowest point in the state is more than half a mile above sea level. (It is in the northeast corner.)

There is too little rain for raising crops in the usual way. Some farmers irrigate their fields. Others do dry farming—using the rainfall of *two* years, stored in the soil, to produce *one* crop. The Great Plains are grassy. The basins of the mountain section are sagebrush country.

Winters are long and cold in Wyoming, especially in the mountainous west. The short summers are hot during daylight hours, but night brings rapid cooling.

History Every museum in Wyoming has a collection of Indian arrowheads found in the state. Some of these arrowheads are thousands of years old. The early Indian peoples left things that puzzle Indians as well as others today. On cliffs and in caves are pictures that no one can understand. Some are painted and some are carved. In the Big Horn Mountains, there is the amazing Medicine Wheel. Its center is a hub of stone, and twenty-eight stone spokes go out from the hub. The wheel is 245 feet (75 m) across. Around its edge are the remains of several low stone shelters. In later times, Crow Indians lived in the Big Horn Mountains.

Part of what is now the state was claimed by Spain in the early days. A large part belonged to France. And part was in the Oregon Territory that

▲ *Bronco riders try their luck at the Cheyenne Frontier Days rodeo in Wyoming.*

Wyoming has weathered rock towers called buttes on its treeless basins. The most famous is Devils Tower which became the first national monument in the United States.

Jim Bridger, a Wyoming scout and fur trapper, built a trading post, Fort Bridger, in 1842. It is gone, but the state park at the site has other old, restored buildings to visit. Stables of the Pony Express and the store of a frontier trader are among them.

▲ *The Teton Mountains in western Wyoming are part of the Grand Teton National Park, established in 1929.*

▼ *The rugged pinnacled landscape of Mammoth Hot Springs in Yellowstone National Park, Wyoming.*

Britain and the United States argued over.

The first American exploration in Wyoming was that of John Colter. He had been a member of the Lewis and Clark party of soldier-explorers. The party did not enter Wyoming, but Colter received permission to leave the others and go there.

In 1807, Colter went trapping in the Big Horn Mountains. Later he passed through the Yellowstone country. When he returned to Saint Louis, he described the geysers he had seen shooting from the ground. Not many people believed what he told them.

For some time, trapping was the chief occupation of the white people in Wyoming. Trappers and soldiers helped the "Westward Movement" by discovering the best routes west. A fur-trading post, later named Fort Laramie, became the earliest lasting settlement in Wyoming.

Thousands of wagons crossed the Rockies through the South Pass, which ran through the valley of the Sweetwater River. Many people were going to California for gold. Others were going to Oregon for rich farmland. Only a few wanted to settle in dry Wyoming. But the discovery of gold and coal in Wyoming changed matters, and so did the discovery that plains grass made good grazing. Settlers began to arrive. The Union Pa-cific Railroad helped them come. The railroad's tracks reached Wyoming in 1867.

The motto of Wyoming is "Equal Rights." Even before Wyoming was a state, it became a leader in the cause of women's rights. The territory was the first to grant women the vote. After 1869, women could also serve on juries. In 1870, South Pass City had the first woman justice of the peace in the United States. The country's first woman governor, Nellie Tayloe Ross, took office in Cheyenne, the capital of Wyoming, in 1925. Mrs. Ross later became director of the U.S. Mint.

Wyoming People at Work Coal lies under much of Wyoming. Only a small part of it has been mined so far. Oil is Wyoming's most important underground resource. The state also has natural gas, iron ore, and uranium. Sand and gravel is extracted for use in construction work. Casper is an oil-refining center. The University of Wyoming is at Laramie.

Ranching is the second biggest business. The main animals bred are cattle and sheep. Since cowboys must ride, horse raising has always been important in Wyoming. The state's leading field crops are wheat, hay, oats, and sugar beets. Manufacturing employs relatively few people.

The mountains and lakes of Grand Teton National Park and the wildlife and geysers of Yellowstone National Park attract many people to Wyoming every year. The nation's first national monument, Devils Tower, is a high volcanic plug in northeastern Wyoming. It can be seen for many miles. National Elk Refuge, covering 25,000 acres (10,000 hectares), is near Jackson and provides winter grazing grounds for thousands of migrating elks.

ALSO READ: GEYSER, GREAT PLAINS, ROCKY MOUNTAINS, SHOSHONE INDIANS, YELLOWSTONE PARK.

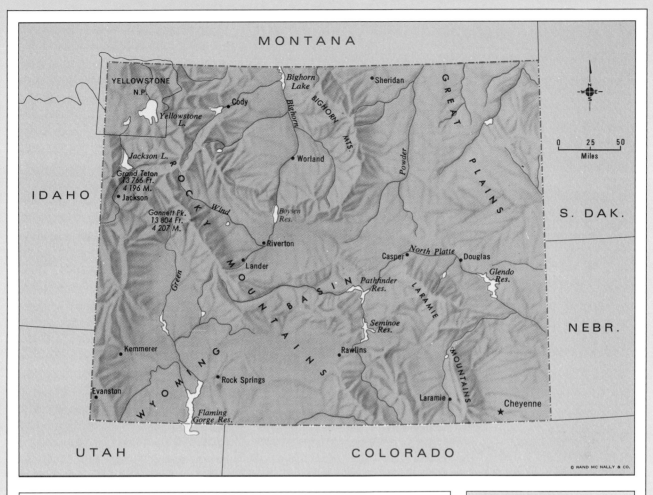

MONTANA

YELLOWSTONE
N.P.

Bighorn
Lake

•Sheridan

G
R
E
A
T

•Cody

Bighorn

BIGHORN
MTS.

Yellowstone
L.

P
L
A
I
N
S

Jackson L.

•Worland

R
O
C
K
Y

Powder

Grand Teton
13,766 Ft.
4,196 M.
•Jackson

IDAHO

S. DAK.

Gannett Pk.
13,804 Ft.
4,207 M.

Wind

Boysen
Res.

M
O
U
N
T
A
I
N
S

•Riverton

Casper•

North Platte

•Douglas

Green

•Lander

Glendo
Res.

Pathfinder
Res.

L
A
R
A
M
I
E

NEBR.

W
Y
O
M
I
N
G

B
A
S
I
N

Seminoe
Res.

•Kemmerer

•Rawlins

M
O
U
N
T
A
I
N
S

•Rock Springs

•Evanston

Laramie•

Cheyenne
★

Flaming
Gorge Res.

UTAH

COLORADO

© RAND MC NALLY & CO.

0   25   50
Miles

STATE EMBLEMS

Cottonwood

Meadowlark

Indian Paintbrush

WYOMING

Capital
Cheyenne (47,000 people)

Area
97,914 square miles (253,358
sq. km). Rank: 9th

Population
509,000 people
Rank: 50th

Statehood
July 10, 1890
44th state admitted

Principal rivers
Bighorn River
Green River
North Platte River

Highest point
Gannet Peak on the
Continental Divide; 13,785
feet (4,202 m)

Largest city
Casper (51,000 people)

Motto
"Equal Rights"

Song
"Wyoming"

Famous people
James Bridger, Buffalo Bill
Cody, Nellie Tayloe Ross

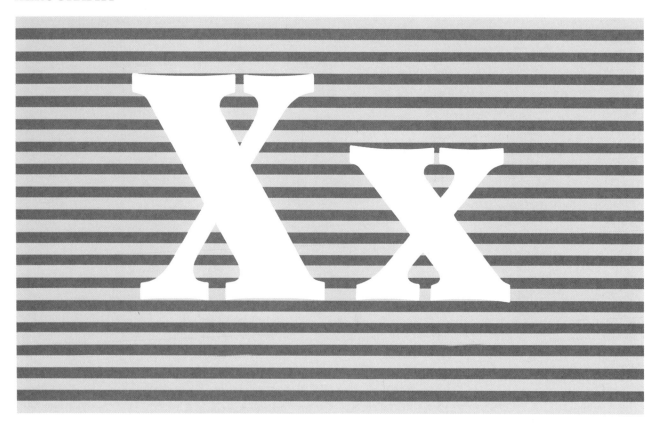

▲ *The Persian king Xerxes I, also called Ahasuerus.*

XERXES I (about 519–465 B.C.) Xerxes I was a king of the ancient Persian Empire. In the book of Esther in the Bible, Xerxes is the mighty king Ahasuerus, who "reigned from India to Ethiopia over 127 provinces." He was a wise ruler as well as a fearful conqueror of other lands.

Xerxes became king after the death of his father, Darius the Great, in 486 B.C. At that time, the Persians were enemies of the Greeks. During Darius' reign, the Athenians had defeated the Persians at the great Battle of Marathon in 490 B.C. Soon after Xerxes became king, he began to plan an invasion of Greece. He gathered together a great army of over 180,000 men and a very large fleet of ships. He built roads and stored food for his armies along the way. He built two bridges of boats moored end to end across the Hellespont strait (now the Dardanelles). He is also said to have dug a canal across the peninsula of Mount Athos.

Xerxes set out in 480 B.C. According to the Greek historian Herodotus, the Persian army numbered nearly three million men. (The actual figure was probably nearer 200,000.) Xerxes defeated the people of the Greek city of Sparta at the Battle of Thermopylae, in 480 B.C. He then marched to Athens and burned the city including all the houses and temples.

But at the Battle of Salamis later that year, the Greek fleet, commanded by the Athenian general Themistocles, defeated the much larger Persian fleet. Xerxes watched the battle from his throne, which had been placed on a nearby hilltop. After the defeat, Xerxes returned to Persia. He left his brother-in-law, Mardonius, in charge of the Persian army in Greece. Mardonius was defeated the following year, 479 B.C. Xerxes gave up his ideas of conquest and was later murdered by his palace guard.

ALSO READ: GREECE, ANCIENT; PERSIA.

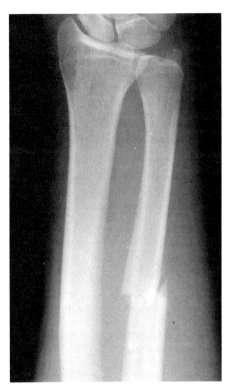

▲ *An X ray of a broken bone. Bone tissue shows up as white or light gray on an X ray.*

X RAY When you go to the dentist, he or she shines a bright light into your mouth. The visible light rays make it possible for the dentist to examine the outside of your teeth. To examine the inside of your teeth, the dentist uses an X-ray machine that sends invisible X rays through your teeth. A piece of photographic film is placed behind the teeth. The X rays make a shadow picture of the teeth on the film.

Light rays and X rays are both forms of electromagnetic radiation. Electromagnetic radiation is caused by the motion of electrical charges. X rays are produced when high-speed electrons (electrically charged bits of matter) strike a solid target. The electrons can produce X rays in two different ways. As electrons are slowed down by the target, their path is bent and energy is given off in the form of X rays. They can also knock other electrons out of the atoms. The remaining electrons jump to fill the gap

and also give off X rays.

The penetrating power of the X rays given off depends on the velocity (speed and direction) of the electrons striking the target. The velocity of the electrons can be changed by changing the voltage (electrical potential) in the X-ray tube. A higher voltage produces faster electrons, and, therefore, more powerful X rays.

A typical X-ray tube is a glass tube that has been *evacuated*—it contains no air or other gases. Inside the glass tube at opposite ends are a *cathode* that gives off electrons and an *anode*, or target, that is hit by the electrons. When the cathode is heated by an electric current to a high temperature, electrons fly off the hot cathode and strike the anode. This action produces X rays and heat.

In medicine, X rays are used both for diagnosis—finding out what is wrong—and treatment. The dentist uses X rays to photograph cavities and other disorders of the teeth. Physicians use X rays to photograph broken bones, tumors, and the effects of certain diseases, such as tuberculosis and pneumonia. The physican may use a fluorescent screen called a *fluoroscope* instead of photographic film. The fluoroscope forms a temporary X-ray image on a screen. Patients who are to be X-rayed sometimes swallow, or are injected with, special dyes or substances that will pass into

▲ *Wilhelm Conrad Roentgen, the German scientist who discovered the X ray.*

▼ *Inside the X-ray machine, a heated filament produces a stream of electrons. These are accelerated toward a metal target. When the electron beam hits the target, X rays are given off by the electrons. The X-ray beam is directed through a window to pass through the patient's body.*

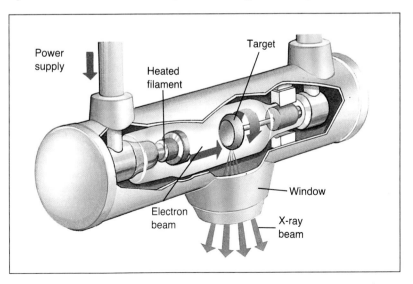

Power supply

Heated filament

Target

Electron beam

Window

X-ray beam

▲ *Ordinary X rays cannot show great internal detail. The X-ray scanner, however, can take a detailed picture of a "slice" through the patient's body. It X-rays the slice from different angles and then uses a computer to calculate tissue thickness within the slice. The result is displayed as a cross-section picture on a screen.*

Not all X rays are man-made. Astronomers have found that X rays are reaching us from outer space. Strange objects in space called quasars throw out enormous amounts of X rays.

their bloodstream, digestive tract, or certain organs. The dyes show conditions that would not otherwise be visible on the X rays.

Although X rays can penetrate all parts of the body, they do not pene-

trate them equally well. Bones, teeth, and other hard parts of the body block more X rays than do organs, muscles, and the softer parts of the body. This is what makes X-ray photographs possible. The more X rays that strike the film, the darker the film will be when it is developed. Flesh appears dark in an X-ray photograph, and bones appear light.

X rays can make people sick or make them well. X rays can destroy healthy tissues and cause unhealthy tissue growth. An overexposure to X rays can cause blood diseases, cancer, and damage to reproductive organs. But X rays can also destroy unhealthy tissue. Because of this, they can be used to treat cancer, which is a

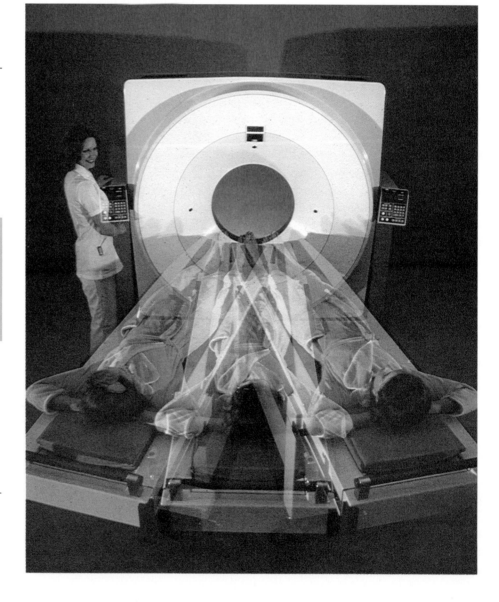

▶ *The patient lies on a couch that moves automatically into the scanner tunnel and is positioned where required beneath the X-ray emitter.*

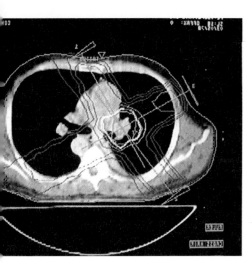

▲ *This scan of a body slice across the chest clearly shows the spine and the rib cage.*

growth of unhealthy tissue in the body.

Scientists use X rays to study the underlying structure of substances. In industry, X rays are used to inspect materials and products, such as metals, plastics, and rubber insulation, in order to discover defects in them before they are put into production. Museums use X rays to examine paintings to identify the artist or period. Sometimes a second painting is discovered underneath the first. X rays can be used in almost any situation where someone wants to see inside something that cannot be penetrated by light.

X rays were discovered in 1895 by the German physicist, Wilhelm Conrad Roentgen. Roentgen was working with cathode rays (electrons) and noticed that when the rays hit the sides of the tube, a nearby fluorescent screen began to glow. The glowing continued, even when a sheet of heavy black paper was placed between the tube and the screen. He could not explain the mysterious rays, so he called them X rays.

ALSO READ: ATOM, CANCER, ELECTRICITY, LIGHT, MEDICINE, RADIATION, RADIOACTIVITY, WAVE.

XYLOPHONE A member of the percussion group of musical intruments, the xylophone has wooden or metal bars that the player strikes with small mallets or hammers. The bars differ in length to sound the notes of several octaves. Metal tubes below the bars are *resonators* that help make a larger, fuller tone.

A *marimba* is a kind of xylophone that uses hollowed gourds as resonators for the wooden bars. This instrument is found in Africa and in Central America. It is especially popular in Guatemala, where some instruments are so large that several persons play on one marimba at the same time. The *vibraphone*, which has metal bars, resembles the marimba.

The xylophone and the *glockenspiel*, a similar instrument, are used in orchestras and concert bands. The glockenspiel has metal bars tuned to the chromatic scale. It is small enough to be carried in marching bands. Simple forms of the xylophone were played in Africa and Asia in ancient times. The instrument is still used in Asian and African folk music. The French composer, Camille Saint-Saëns, used the xylophone in his *Danse Macabre* to suggest the rattling bones of dancing skeletons.

ALSO READ: MUSIC, MUSICAL INSTRUMENTS, ORCHESTRAS AND BANDS, PERCUSSION INSTRUMENTS.

A large xylophone with a resonator, or echo chamber, is called a marimba. This was originally of African origin. A modern version of this, often used by jazz musicians, is the vibraphone, or vibes as it is more familiarly known.

▼ *The xylophone has wooden or metal bars and is played with small mallets or hammers. The sound is reinforced by resonators hanging beneath the bars.*

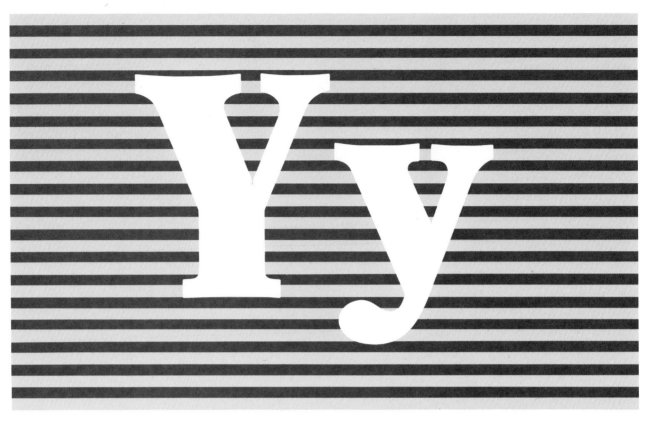

YANGTZE RIVER The Yangtze is the longest river in China. It flows about 3,400 miles (5,472 km), from the snow-covered Himalaya Mountains of Tibet (now a region of China) to the East China Sea near Shanghai. (See the map with the article on CHINA.) The Yangtze, or *Ch'ang Ji-ang* ("long river") as the Chinese call it, is the major river of central China.

Near its start, the Yangtze flows southward through deep gorges cut into the high mountains. The river then turns northeastward and flows past Chungking. The Chinese Nationalists made this city their capital while they fought to control China during the 1940's. Beyond Chungking, the Yangtze rushes through the spectacular Yangtze Gorges, which are perilous to shipping. The river then winds through a lowland agricultural region to the sea.

Shanghai, China's largest city, grew as a major port near the mouth of the Yangtze. Nanking, farther upstream, is an important industrial center with iron, steel, and silk mills. Oceangoing ships can travel upstream as far as Wu-han, a distance of about 600 miles (965 km). Riverboats can travel about 600 miles farther to Chungking.

During spring floods, the amount of water in the Yangtze sometimes doubles. The river often overflows, flooding cropland and destroying lives and property.

ALSO READ: CHINA, RIVER.

▼ *The powerful current of the Yangtze River is clearly evident here, beneath the impressive slopes of the Yangtze Gorges.*

YEAST A yeast is a plant. The whole plant is made up of one cell, so small that you need a microscope to see it. A yeast is a *fungus*, a plant that cannot make its own food. Yeasts live on sugar. Yeast cells excrete *enzymes*, which change sugar to alcohol and carbon dioxide gas.

New yeast plants are formed by "budding." Part of the plant pushes outward. This part later breaks off and becomes a separate yeast plant.

Great numbers of yeast cells, in the form of a paste, are mixed into bread dough. The yeast enzymes change the sugar in the bread dough to alcohol and carbon dioxide. The carbon dioxide forms thousands of bubbles in the dough. The bubbles make the dough rise—make it light and fluffy. The many holes you see in a slice of bread are the remains of the bubbles. The alcohol evaporates in the heat of the baking oven. Another kind of yeast is used to make beer and ale.

■ LEARN BY DOING

Buy a package of yeast or a yeast cake at the supermarket. Dissolve a spoonful of sugar in a glass of warm water. Drop into the water a small amount of yeast. Place the glass in sunlight. In a few minutes, you will see bubbles of carbon dioxide rising from the yeast. ■

ALSO READ: BAKING AND BAKERIES, ENZYME, FERMENTATION, FUNGUS.

YELLOW RIVER The Yellow River is the main waterway of northern China. It flows for more than 3,000 miles (4,800 km) and is the second longest river in China, after the Yangtze (See the map with the article on CHINA). The Chinese call this important river *Hwang Ho*, Chinese for "yellow river."

The Yellow River rises in the Himalaya Mountains of Tibet (now a region of China). Leaving the moun-

tains, the river flows in a great bend to the north and east, skirting the Ordos Desert. For its last 400 miles (644 km), the river flows across a broad plain to empty into the Yellow Sea. It gets its name from the yellowish soil carried downstream.

The mouth of the Yellow River has actually changed location. A century ago, this river emptied into the East China Sea, south of the Shantung Peninsula. About 1853, natural causes shifted the flow to the north of the Shangtung Peninsula, where the river mouth lies today.

The sediment carried by the Yellow River builds up sandbars and makes navigation difficult. No large port city stands at the mouth of the river. The Yellow River is called "China's Sorrow" because of the many times it has overflowed, ruining crops and homes. For hundreds of years, the Chinese have tried to control the floods by building dikes, or high banks, alongside the river.

ALSO READ: CHINA, RIVER.

YELLOWSTONE PARK Yellowstone Park is the largest national park in the United States. It covers more than two million acres (800,000 hectares), mostly in Wyoming, but extending into Montana and Idaho as well.

▲ *Soil erosion is much in evidence along the banks of the Yellow River. This is caused by terrible seasonal flooding.*

Yeasts contain many vitamins. They are particularly rich in vitamins of the B group.

2633

▲ *The famous geyser "Old Faithful" is one of many geysers and hot springs in Yellowstone National Park. The geyser spouts steam, which is produced by water that seeps down through the rock and is heated by volcanic activity underground.*

More than 200 active geysers can be found in the park. The most famous geyser is called Old Faithful. It erupts on the average every 65 minutes, shooting a column of hot water and a cloud of water vapor 120 to 170 feet (36 to 52 m) into the air. Giant Geyser sends hot water 250 feet (76 m) into the air but is not as predictable as Old Faithful.

About 3,000 hot springs cover the geyser basins of the park. The minerals contained in those hot waters form brightly colored cones and other formations on surrounding land. Mud volcanoes bubble like hot fudge on a stove in some areas.

The Yellowstone River cuts the park in two. It descends into yellowstone's Grand Canyon in two spectacular waterfalls. In the canyon, steep walls display the yellow color that gives the river and park its name. The river also passes through Yellowstone Lake, one of the highest bodies of water of its size in North America.

Yellowstone is an important wildlife refuge. Wapiti (North American elk), moose, coyotes, pronghorn antelope, porcupines, skunks, bighorn sheep, mink, otter, badgers, grizzly bears, and weasels thrive there. Hunting is forbidden in the park, but camping, hiking, and horseback riding are permitted.

Yellowstone was discovered in 1807 by an American trapper named John Colter. No one believed his descriptions of Yellowstone's amazing phenomena until 1870, when a government expedition reported that the stories were true. Yellowstone became the country's first national park in 1872.

ALSO READ: GEYSER, NATIONAL PARK.

YEMEN   see ARABIA.

YIDDISH LANGUAGE   Few languages match Yiddish in colorfulness and adaptability. It originated in the A.D. 900's, when Jewish immigrants in Germany learned to speak German but used the Hebrew alphabet to write it. They added Hebrew words to their speech which they "Germanized." Although frowned upon by Jewish religious leaders as slang, this dialect gradually took shape as a language separate from German. Years later when Jewish colonies in Germany moved to Poland and Russia, Yiddish survived and grew, adopting many words from Polish and Russian. America has also played an important role in the development of Yiddish. Large numbers of Jews came from Europe around 1882, bringing with them their Yiddish language. Here their language was further enriched with English words, especially the names of things unfamiliar to the immigrants, such as *ice cream*, *subway*, and *baseball*. English has also been enriched by colorful Yiddish expressions, such as *bagel*, *schlemiel*, and *kibitzer*.

Yiddish may be a vanishing language for several reasons. Several million Yiddish-speaking Jews were killed in Europe during the 1930's and during World War II. Hebrew, not Yiddish, is the official language of Israel. In North and South America, the number of new Jewish immigrants is small, and new generations tend to drop the language.

ALSO READ: GERMAN LANGUAGE, JEWISH HISTORY, LANGUAGES.

YOGA   To many people, yoga means a form of meditation, or deep thought, practiced in association with certain physical exercises. Yoga is an Eastern philosophy, developed by the Hindus of India. The person wishing to practice Yoga must train both body and mind and pass through certain stages until he or she reaches a state of release from the everyday world.

Yoga is a very ancient philosophy.

▲ *Indians practice their Yoga in Varanasi (Benares), a famous Hindu city on the Ganges River.*

It involves high levels of mental concentration and considerable practice. One way in which people may free themselves from the "distractions" of the world is by exercises in posture and breathing. These exercises, developed by the school of Hatha Yoga, are also practiced by those people who merely seek to relax and to improve their physical condition. This form of Yoga is practiced in many parts of the world besides India. Practicing Yoga makes the body more flexible and tones up the muscles. However, it is unwise for a beginner to attempt Yoga without instruction from an expert.

ALSO READ: HINDUISM.

YOM KIPPUR Yom Kippur is the most solemn holy day of the Jewish faith. It is also called the Day of Atonement. It comes at the end of the Ten Penitential Days, which begin with Rosh Hashanah, the Jewish New Year. Yom Kippur falls in September or early October, on the tenth day of Tishri, the first month of the Hebrew calendar. It actually begins at sundown of the ninth day.

Many Jewish people *fast* (do not have anything to eat or drink, even water) until sundown of the next day. During that time they pray and attend services. The services begin with a beautiful hymn called the *Kol Nidre*. Jewish people pray that they may be forgiven for their sins, both by God and by anyone whom they may have hurt during the year. At the end of the day, a trumpet called the *shofar*, made from a ram's horn, is blown. It makes a long, mournful sound and tells the people that Yom Kippur is over.

ALSO READ: JUDAISM.

YORK, HOUSE OF see ENGLISH HISTORY, WARS OF THE ROSES.

YOSEMITE VALLEY The Yosemite Valley is a narrow gorge in central California, about 200 miles (320 km) east of San Francisco. This spectacular valley in the Sierra Nevada mountain range is only about 7 miles (11 km) long and 1 mile (1.6 km) wide.

Yosemite Valley was made a California state park in 1864. California gave the land to the Federal Government in 1906, and it became part of Yosemite National Park. The park now covers about 760,000 acres (307,000 hectares). It has spectacular waterfalls, unusual rock formations, and high, rugged mountains.

The park has other attractions in addition to the Yosemite Valley, but the valley is the most scenic area. Steep granite walls surround the valley, which is carpeted with evergreen trees. El Capitán, a massive granite mountain, rises 3,604 feet (1,098 m) from the valley floor. Several waterfalls, including Ribbon Fall (1,612 feet / 491 m) and Bridalveil Fall (620 feet / 189 m) pour into the valley. The highest waterfall is Yosemite Falls (2,425 feet / 739 m). It consists of the

▲ *The shofar, a ram's horn, is blown to signify the end of Yom Kippur, the Day of Atonement. Moses, the great leader of the Jews, set Yom Kippur as the most sacred day almost 3,000 years ago.*

The Indians who settled in the valley were of the Miwok tribe. They were called Yosemite, which is Miwok for "grizzly bear," after their clan totem.

▲ *Yosemite National Park is a region of clear sparkling lakes and jagged mountain peaks.*

▲ *Andrew Young, diplomat and political figure.*

▲ *Brigham Young, Mormon leader.*

Upper Yosemite Fall (1,430 feet / 436 m), and Lower Yosemite Fall (320 feet / 98 m), with a series of cascades, which cover 675 feet (206 m), in between. The best time to see the falls is in May or June. By the end of the summer, they may dry up from lack of melting snow and rain.

Yosemite includes three groves of giant sequoia trees. The largest tree has a diameter of about 35 feet (11 m) at its base and a height of 209 feet (64 m). It is estimated to be about 3,800 years old. Black bears and mule deer roam the park. So do marmots, ground squirrels, and porcupines. More than 700 miles (1,125 km) of hiking and horsebackriding trails wind through Yosemite. A park museum provides exhibits of plant and animal life and of the history of the local Indians.

ALSO READ: CALIFORNIA, NATIONAL PARK, SIERRA NEVADA.

YOUNG, ANDREW (born 1932) Andrew Young has been a civil rights leader, U.S. Congressman, and U.S. ambassador to the United Nations. He was born in New Orleans, Louisiana, and studied at Howard University, in Washington, D.C. He then turned to the church and became an aide to Martin Luther King, Jr. In 1972, Young was the first black elected to Congress from a district in Atlanta, Georgia.

Young was an effective Congressman, and in 1977, he was appointed by President Carter to be U.S. ambassador to the United Nations. His support for Third World nations aroused controversy, and in 1979, he resigned after charges that he had had a secret meeting at the U.N. with the Palestine Liberation Organization. In 1981, Young was elected mayor of Atlanta.

ALSO READ: KING, MARTIN LUTHER, JR.

YOUNG, BRIGHAM (1801–1877) Brigham Young was a leader of the Morman church, officially called the Church of Jesus Christ of the Latter-day Saints. He helped settle what is now the state of Utah.

Young was born in Whitingham, Vermont. As a young man, he worked as a carpenter and a painter in western New York. Young was raised a Methodist but was converted to Mormonism in 1832. Three years later, he became a member of the Quorum of the Twelve Apostles, the ruling body of the Mormon Church. For several years afterward, Young traveled through parts of the United States and Britain, serving as a missionary. When Joseph Smith, the founder of Mormonism, was murdered in 1844, Young became the head of the church.

Young planned and supervised a westward migration of 5,000 Mormons in 1846. He chose their settlement place at the site of what is now Salt Lake City, Utah. Under Young's leadership, the community prospered. In 1850, when the region became the Territory of Utah, Young was made governor. However, he was removed from office in 1857 after he publicly endorsed polygamy (having more than one husband or wife).

ALSO READ: LATTER-DAY SAINTS; SMITH, JOSEPH; UTAH.

YOUNG, WHITNEY MOORE, JR. (1921–1971)

Whitney Young was an American civil rights leader who devoted most of his life to helping other black people in the United States.

Young was born in Lincoln Ridge, Kentucky. He studied at Kentucky State College and the University of Minnesota. In 1947, he joined the National Urban League, an organization that works to give black people in the United States the same opportunities as white people in housing, jobs, and education. Young served as industrial relations director for the branch of the Urban League in Saint Paul, Minnesota, until 1950. He then became executive secretary of the Omaha branch in Nebraska.

In 1954, Young was appointed dean of the School of Social Work at Atlanta University. He left that position in 1961 to become executive director of the National Urban League at its headquarters in New York City. Young set up many programs to encourage young people to train for the careers of their choice. He served on several Presidential commissions investigating social problems in the United States. Young wrote the books *To Be Equal* and *Beyond Racism*. In 1969, he was awarded the Medal of Freedom, the highest civilian award in the United States.

ALSO READ: CIVIL RIGHTS MOVEMENT.

YOUNG PEOPLE'S ASSOCIATIONS

Many young people enjoy belonging to an association, club, or movement that provides recreational activities, outdoor adventure, and the chance to learn new skills and games and make new friends. For example, in 1980 there were over a million American boys who belonged to Boys' Clubs. The national organization of the Boys' Clubs of America was started in 1906.

Camp Fire Girls This organization was founded in 1910. Its symbol is a flame and crossed logs. Camp Fire Girls are organized in four age groups: Blue Birds (7 and 8), Camp Fire Girls (9 through 11), Junior Hi Camp Girls (12 and 13), and Horizon Club (14 and over). Members are guided by leaders in programs of service to the community and country, and learn skills in homemaking and outdoor life.

Four-H Club Have you ever wished you knew how to repair a bicycle, raise chickens, preserve foods, or make clothes? Members of a Four-H, or 4-H, Club learn all these skills and more. Anyone between the ages of 9 and 19 can join 4-H, which began in the American farmlands in the early 1900's. Today, only about a fourth of all 4-H members in the United States live on farms. More than 80 countries around the world have 4-H organizations. The United States Department of Agriculture in Washington, D.C., has information on 4-H Clubs throughout the country.

Scouts The international Scout movement began with the founding of the Boy Scouts by a British army officer, Robert Baden-Powell. In 1907, he organized a boys' camp, and in 1908 he wrote a handbook of activities called *Scouting for Boys*. William D. Boyce and Daniel Beard founded

▲ *Whitney M. Young, Jr., civil rights leader.*

▼ *These young people are crossing the fast-flowing waters of the Wind River in Wyoming. Expeditions for young persons, such as this one, are well supervised by adults.*

▲ *These Boy Scouts in Philadelphia are dressed in their uniforms. They have worked hard to earn their badges.*

the Boy Scout movement in the United States. Boy Scouts are aged 11 to 17 and meet in patrols, several of which form a troop. Boys aged 8 to 10 are *Cub Scouts.*

Girl Scouts are called Girl Guides in some countries. The first U.S. troop was organized by Juliette Gordon Low in Savannah, Georgia. Girl Scouts are organized in four age groups. *Brownies* are 6 through 8. *Junior Girl Scouts* are 9 through 11. *Cadettes* are 12 through 14, and *Senior Girl Scouts* are 15 through 17.

Boy and Girl Scouts all over the world make a pledge, or promise. They share the motto "Be Prepared" and the slogan "Do a Good Turn Daily." The Scout movement promotes international friendship and community service. Camping and conservation are favorite activities. Scouts are awarded badges for achievement in various skills.

YMCA and YWCA The Young Men's Christian Association (YMCA or simply the "Y") was founded in England by George Williams in 1844, mainly for Bible study and prayer. Today, anyone, of whatever religious belief, can join, though most "Y" members are boys and men under 25. Teenagers can join Hi-Y Clubs.

Most YMCA buildings display the "Y" symbol, a red triangle. They often have cafeterias, residence halls, and sports facilities. The YMCA also sponsors educational classes, craft workshops, and hobby centers.

The Young Women's Christian Association (YWCA) was founded in England in 1855. The first U.S. YWCA was founded in New York City in 1858. Girls can join Y-Teen Clubs aged 12 through 18. Men and boys can become associate members.

YUGOSLAVIA The Socialist Federal Republic of Yugoslavia lies along the Adriatic Sea in southeastern Europe. This country is composed of six republics—Serbia (which includes the autonomous provinces of Kosovo and Vojvodina), Croatia, Bosnia-Hercegovina, Slovenia, Macedonia, and Montenegro. Yugoslavia is the largest country of the Balkan Peninsula. (See the map with the article on EUROPE.) The name Yugoslavia means "Land of the Southern Slavs." Ancestors of the Yugoslav people were *Slavs*, tribes that came from the north a thousand years ago.

Mountains and highlands cover most of Yugoslavia. The Dinaric Alps along the coast are the chief mountain range. Dalmatia, the Adriatic coastal plain, is a beautiful place with a warm climate and many islands lying off the coastline. Dubrovnik and Split are old medieval cities, popular with vacationers. The Danube River waters a fertile plain that supports farms and orchards. On a hill overlooking the Danube lies Belgrade, the capital.

The Yugoslav peoples, although closely related, differ from each other

YUGOSLAVIA

Capital City: Belgrade (1,470,000 people).
Area: 98,774 square miles (255,804 sq. km).
Population: 23,100,000.
Government: Federal republic.
Natural Resources: Coal, iron, copper, lead, chrome.
Export Products: Machinery, electrical goods, transport equipment, chemicals.
Unit of Money: Dinar.
Official Languages: Serbo-Croat, Slovene, Macedonian.

in religion and language. The main groups of people are Serbs, Croats, Slovenes, Macedonians, and the Montenegrins of the isolated mountain regions. There are three major languages—Serbo-Croat, Slovene, and Macedonian.

Yugoslavia is rich in minerals, such as coal, and copper, and also in forests that supply lumber. All industry is owned by the state. Textiles, chemicals, and electrical equipment are manufactured. Zagreb is a leading industrial city.

Many farmers work their own little plots. Others work on big, modern farms owned by the state. The main crops are corn, wheat, barley, and rye. Grapes, oranges, and lemons grow along the coast, where tourism is important.

Yugoslavia became a nation in 1918. It was ruled by a king. Before World War I, Serbia and Montenegro were independent countries, and the rest of the country was part of the Austro-Hungarian Empire. During World War II, German troops occupied the country, and Yugoslav partisans (resistance fighters) fought against them.

After the war, a Communist partisan leader, Josip Broz, or Marshal Tito as he was called, was in control. Yugoslavia was declared to be a Communist people's republic. After Tito's death in 1980, a collective presidency, rotating among the presidents of Yugoslavia's republics and provinces, went into effect.

ALSO READ: ADRIATIC SEA, DANUBE RIVER, TITO.

YUKON TERRITORY The Yukon Territory is a wild, rugged region of Canada in the far northwest corner of the country. The state of Alaska lies along its western border. The Yukon Territory is about twice the size of Colorado, but the Yukon has less than one-hundredth the number of people of that state.

The Yukon lies on a high plateau, stretching south from the Arctic Ocean. More than 20 peaks in the territory rise higher than 10,000 feet (3,000 m). At 19,850 feet (6,050 m), Mount Logan is the highest mountain in Canada. The Yukon River, one of North America's longest rivers, runs across the southern part of the territory. Winters in the Yukon are long and very cold. The land is covered with deep snow for much of the year. During the short summers, some hardy grains and vegetables are grown in some southern regions of the Yukon.

Most of the people work in mining, logging, tourism, or government activities. The territory has deposits of silver, copper, lead, nickel, asbestos, zinc, oil, and natural gas. There are valuable forests of white spruce and pine. Some of the local Indians are fur traders. Muskrat, beaver, and other fur-bearing animals live in the Yukon. The chief cities are Faro, Watson Lake, Dawson, and Whitehorse, the capital.

A British expedition led by Sir John Franklin explored the Yukon's Arctic coast in the 1820's. Fur-trading posts were later set up by the Hudson's Bay Company, which sold its rights to the territory to the Canadian government in 1870.

In 1896, gold was discovered around the Klondike River in central Yukon. Prospectors and miners from all over North America flocked to the Klondike region and the rest of the territory to seek their fortunes. By 1910, most of the gold had been exhausted and many people had left. In the 1940's, thousands of workers went there when part of the Alaska Highway was built in the Yukon. The Canadian government has since encouraged the development of permanent industries in Yukon Territory.

ALSO READ: CANADA, GOLD RUSH, HUDSON'S BAY COMPANY.

▲ *Dubrovnik is a medieval city and port on Yugoslavia's Adriatic coast. It is a popular tourist resort.*

The Yugoslavian seaport of Split is an ancient Roman town. Here, the vast palace of the Emperor Diocletian is one of the most impressive ruins in the ancient world. Its walls are 7 feet (2 m) thick and 72 feet (22 m) high on the seaward side.

At the peak of the gold rush to the Yukon's Klondike, more than 30,000 people moved into the territory. In the year 1900, gold worth $22 million was found in the area.

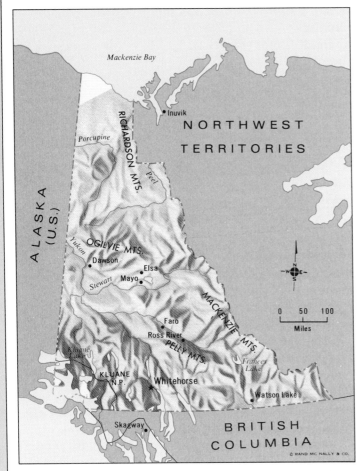

▲ *Dawson is one of the chief cities of the Yukon, but its population, like those of other Yukon cities, is small. The Yukon Territory's total population is only 23,000.*

▲ *The Yukon River runs across the south of the Yukon Territory in Canada. It is one of North America's longest rivers.*

▲ *Several settlements border the Klondike River.*

YUKON TERRITORY

Capital and largest city
Whitehorse (17,600 people)

Area
184,931 square miles
(478,934 sq. km)

Population
23,000 people

Yukon Territory created
1898

Principal river
Yukon

Highest point
Mt. Logan; 19,850 feet
(6,050 m)

PROVINCIAL FLOWER

Fireweed

ZAIRE The big African country of Zaire was once known as Congo Free State—a colony of Belgium. The country received its independence from Belgium in 1960 and took the name Zaire in 1971.

Zaire is the third largest country in Africa—a quarter the size of the United States. Its western neighbor is Congo (Brazzaville). The Central African Republic and the Sudan lie to the north. Uganda, Rwanda, Burundi, and Tanzania are on the east. Zambia and Angola are its southern neighbors. A small stretch of land forms the Atlantic coastline in the southwest. (See the map with the article on AFRICA.)

Much of the country lies in the basin of the Zaire, or Congo River. This region is surrounded by highlands on the west and south. Mountains lie east of the basin. Zaire's climate is a moist, tropical one because of its location on the equator. Rain falls all year in the river area. The rest of the country has a dry season and a rainy season.

The country is rich in minerals. It

ZAIRE

Capital City: Kinshasa (1,855,000 people).

Area: 905,633 square miles (2,345,409 sq. km).

Population: 33,100,000.

Government: Republic.

Natural Resources: Copper, zinc, cobalt, diamonds, timber.

Export Products: Copper, coffee, diamonds, cobalt.

Unit of Money: Zaire.

Official Language: French.

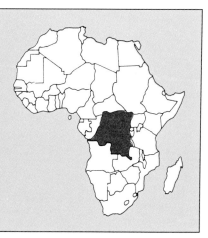

▲ *The Lake Kivu district lies to the far east of Zaire, on the border with Rwanda.*

The Zaire River separates the world's two closest capital cities. People can take a ferry across the river from Kinshasa, the capital of Zaire, to Brazzaville, the capital of the Congo.

is the world's largest producer of industrial diamonds and cobalt, and one of the leading exporters of copper. Coal, manganese, tin, zinc, and gold are also mined. Most of these resources are located in the southeastern section of the country.

Over half the population belongs to various tribal groups speaking Bantu languages. The remainder are members of tribal groups that speak Sudanese or Nilotic languages.

Belgium control over Zaire began in the 1880's. King Leopold II of Belgium claimed the area after hearing about it from the explorer Henry M. Stanley. It was turned over to Belgium in 1908.

The Belgians trained many Zairians in mining and technical jobs before independence. The Belgians, however, took much from the land and educated few people for government jobs and professions. The period following independence was filled with bloodshed. Moise Tshombe, Patrice Lumumba, and Joseph Kasavubu all tried unsuccessfully to lead the country. Joseph Désiré Mobutu finally seized power in 1965.

As part of a plan to go back to older and more authentic (real) names, the name of the country was changed by Mobutu from the Congo to Zaire in late 1971. Zaire was what Portuguese explorers in the 1500's had called the Congo River. The city of Stanleyville

is now Kisangani, and Leopoldville is Kinshasa. President Mobutu took the name of Mobutu Sese Seko.

ALSO READ: AFRICA.

ZAIRE RIVER The Zaire, or Congo, River stretches about 2,900 miles (4,700 km) through central Africa. It flows in a giant semicircle through the lowlands of Zaire and empties into the Atlantic Ocean. The Zaire is the second longest river in Africa—only the Nile is longer—and one of the longest rivers in the world. (See the map with the article on AFRICA.)

The Zaire flows through thick forest, open grasslands called savannas, and marshes near the Atlantic coast. The heavy rainfall of the tropical forest adds water to the river. In fact, the Zaire carries more water to the ocean than any other river does, except the Amazon of South America.

The Zaire is an important means of communication for the people of central Africa. Barges and large ships carry many different cargoes between the inland areas and the coast. The river is divided into three natural parts. The Upper Zaire is shallow, with rapids and waterfalls. The Middle Zaire includes Stanley Pool, a lake formed where the river widens. Livingstone Falls form the mouth of the lake. The two largest cities on the

▼ *A view of the Zaire (Congo) River, the river that drains west-central Africa.*

ZAMBIA

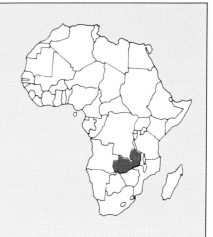

Capital City: Lusaka (538,000 people).
Area: 290,607 square miles (752,614 sq. km).
Population: 7,700,000.
Government: Republic.
Natural Resources: Copper, zinc, lead, coal, cobalt, hydroelectric power.
Export Products: Copper.
Unit of Money: Kwacha.
Official Language: English.

river—Kinshasa and Brazzaville, each the capital of a country—lie near Livingstone Falls. The Lower Zaire stretches from these falls to the Atlantic Ocean. The port of Matadi lies on the Lower Zaire.

European explorers first named the river "Zaire," meaning "river." In the 1600's the name "Congo" was adopted, from the name of a local African kingdom.

ALSO READ: CONGO; LIVINGSTONE, DAVID; RIVER; STANLEY, HENRY MORTON; ZAIRE.

ZAMBIA The Republic of Zambia, formerly the British protectorate of Northern Rhodesia, is a landlocked country located in south-central Africa. It is about twice the size of Montana. Zambia is surrounded by Zaire, Tanzania, Malawi, Mozambique, Zimbabwe, Botswana, Namibia, and Angola. (See the map with the article on AFRICA.) The Zambezi River forms Zambia's border with Zimbabwe. The Kariba Dam project provides hydroelectric power, shared with Zimbabwe. Victoria Falls on the river is wider than Niagara and more than twice its height.

Most of Zambia lies on a fairly high plateau covered with thin forest and grass, making it suitable for both farming and grazing. It is rich in

minerals and is one of the world's largest producers of copper. Other minerals mined there are zinc, cobalt, lead, and manganese.

Many Zambians still make their living as farmers. They grow corn, peanuts, and tobacco. They follow their traditional religions, although many of them are Christian. The capital city is Lusaka (Livingstone was the capital until 1935). Lusaka is a modern, busy city and has an international airport. Other cities are Kitwe and Ndola.

Before Europeans came to Zambia, people had migrated for several hundred years from the Congo River basin toward the south of Africa. These Bantu-speaking people took over the area formerly occupied by Bushmen and other groups. The first non-

▼ *Lake Kariba (visible in the distance) forms the border between Zambia and Zimbabwe. The lake was formed by the construction of the Kariba Dam, which supplies power to Zambia and Zimbabwe.*

Africans to go there were Portuguese explorers and Arab traders.

During the 1850's and 1860's, the British missionary David Livingstone explored the territory. Later the British South Africa Company acquired mineral rights from Lewanika, ruler of the Lozi people, in what is now Zambia and Zimbabwe. Cecil Rhodes handled this operation on behalf of Britain. Northern Rhodesia became a British protectorate in 1924 and became fully independent on October 24, 1964. Zambia was Britain's first dependency to become a republic immediately upon independence. It took the name of Zambia from the Zambezi River. Kenneth Kaunda has been president since 1964.

ALSO READ: AFRICA; RHODES, CECIL; ZIMBABWE.

ZEBRA Zebras are members of the horse family. They range over much of eastern and southern Africa. There are three different types of zebra, distinguished mainly by the arrangement and color of their stripes. One of the most common types, Burchell's zebra, has a light yellow coat with bold black stripes over its whole body. Fainter markings, called shadow stripes, sometime show up between the black stripes. The zebra's stripes, a form of camouflage, make the animal very difficult to see in the shadowy tall grass of an African plain. All zebras have a tufted tail and a short mane that stands erect.

Zebras roam in herds, or groups, grazing on grass and leaves. Each herd is led by a stallion, or male zebra. Female zebras usually have one offspring, or foal, every two or three years. Zebras will kick and bite savagely if attacked. Their main natural enemy is the lion, which hunts them for food. A zebra herd will gallop off at great speed when a lion charges. If a foal cannot run fast enough, its mother will stay behind and defend it to the death. Some kinds of zebras have become almost extinct because of hunters who slaughtered them for their hides. An example of this was the quagga, a zebra which had stripes only on its head and neck.

ZIMBABWE The Republic of Zimbabwe, formerly called Rhodesia, is a landlocked country in south-central Africa. It is slightly smaller in size than California. Harare (formerly Salisbury), the capital, and Bulawayo are the largest cities in Zimbabwe.

Most of Zimbabwe is a high, rolling plateau. The land is largely *veld*, or grassland, with shrub trees. The Zambezi River flows between Zambia and Zimbabwe in the north, and the Limpopo River forms Zimbabwe's

▼ *Zebras drinking at a waterhole in Africa. The zebra's stripes are distinctive, yet they provide good camouflage on the grasslands that are home to these fleet-footed relatives of the horse.*

▼ *A tobacco farm in Zimbabwe. Growing tobacco is one of the country's leading industries.*

ZIMBABWE

Capital City: Harare (656,000 people).
Area: 150,815 square miles (390,580 sq. km).
Population: 10,000,000.
Government: Republic.
Natural Resources: Asbestos, gold, chrome, nickel, coal.
Export Products: Tobacco, minerals, cotton lint, sugar.
Unit of Money: Zimbabwe dollar.
Official Language: English.

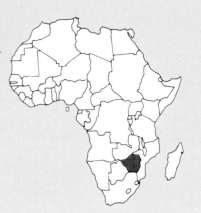

southern border with South Africa.

Zimbabwe has rich farmland, on which tobacco (the country's main crop), sugarcane, cotton, and corn are grown. Beef cattle are raised on the veld. The country has rich mineral resources, including gold, copper, coal, chrome, nickel, and asbestos.

As is shown by the massive stone ruins of Great Zimbabwe, people have settled in this part of Africa since ancient times. In 1889, the Bantu-speaking people of the region gave the British South Africa Company, operated by Cecil Rhodes, permission to begin mining operations and colonization there. The region became the British colony of Southern Rhodesia in 1923. After a short federation with Northern Rhodesia (now Zambia) and Nyasaland (now Malawi), Southern Rhodesia declared its independence from Britain in 1965. It became the nation of Rhodesia, with a white-minority government. Britain called this declaration of independence illegal, and the United Nations imposed economic sanctions. Guerrilla warfare between black nationalists and the whites disrupted the country until late 1979. Then a new constitution, guaranteeing blacks rights, was agreed upon. In 1980, Rhodesia was officially renamed Zimbabwe, with Prime Minister Robert Mugabe as head of a black majority government.

ALSO READ: AFRICA; RHODES, CECIL; SANCTIONS.

ZODIAC see ASTROLOGY, CONSTELLATION.

ZOO The word "zoo" is short for zoological garden. Both terms mean places where live animals are kept on display. People visit zoos just for fun or to learn about different kinds of animals. Modern zoos also make a big contribution to science. *Zoologists* (scientists who study animals) learn by studying animals in zoos, although scientists learn most about animal behavior from observing animals in their natural environment.

There are more than 500 zoos throughout the world. Some large cities, such as New York City, have more than one zoo. But not all zoos are in big cities. Some are in the country, where the animals can have more room. Some are "breeding zoos." Here, groups of wild animals are kept for breeding to raise new populations. Some animals might become extinct if breeding zoos did not help produce new generations. The largest zoo collection is at the San Diego Zoo in California. The National Zoological Park in Washington, D.C., has more than three million visitors a year.

Many modern zoos do not keep all their animals in cages with bars. They have out-of-doors fields, or enclosures. The enclosures are surrounded by *moats*, or wide ditches. Other zoos

▲ *Much time and care are needed to provide the birds in a well-run zoo with a natural, healthy diet.*

The oldest existing zoo is London Zoo in England, owned by the Zoological Society of London. It is also one of the world's largest, housing about 10,000 animals.

▲ *Penguins gather around their keeper, eager to receive a fish. Many zoo animals grow so used to humans that they lose their fear of being approached or even handled.*

▼ *These children are watching an experienced zookeeper handling a python.*

find ways to let people go in with the animals. Enormous flight cages for birds, known as *aviaries*, have pathways, ponds, trees, and bushes. In Jungleworld at the Bronx Zoo, New York, visitors walk through an artificial rain forest. In some country zoos, visitors wander among herds of tame llamas, deer, and other animals. Many zoos include special children's zoos, with animals that can be petted, fed, or even ridden.

Zoos existed in ancient times. A powerful Egyptian queen named Hatshepsut had a zoo in 1400 B.C. The Roman emperors kept animals brought back from all parts of the Roman Empire and beyond. The oldest zoo in the United States is the Philadelphia Zoo, which opened in 1874.

Keeping Animals Healthy   Zoo animals usually live longer than their cousins in the wild. They do not starve or go without water, as wild animals sometimes do. *Veterinarians* care for the health of zoo animals. They give inoculations against diseases and help to plan healthful diets. They trim hoofs or claws and care for skin and teeth. They even perform surgery on sick animals.

SPECIAL NEEDS.   Animal behavior experts know that zoo animals—just like people—need activities to keep them alert and happy. Experiments in one zoo proved that monkeys became

unhappy when the zoo put in special kinds of one-way glass that kept the monkeys from seeing people. But there are limits to the activities a zoo can supply. A lion might feel happier if it could kill a wild zebra, but a zoo could not allow this. Behavior experts have discovered interesting substitutes for the activities that satisfy wild animals; for example, by giving chimpanzees games to play.

Old-fashioned zoos had small cages in which the animals could not get enough exercise to stay well and alert. Modern zoos try to allow each animal the amount of space it likes. Some zoo animals would actually be unhappy in a very large cage or in a big field. In zoos, where food and water are provided, they may feel secure in a small space. Animals that need cool climates live in air-conditioned cages. Animals that need trees are kept in areas containing trees. Aquariums, tanks containing fish and other marine life, are often part of a zoo.

Feeding the Animals   Every animal must have its own diet. Certain snakes will eat only live food, such as mice. Koalas from Australia will eat only fresh eucalyptus leaves.

Zoos plan substitute foods with care. For big cats, such as leopards and tigers, the zoo buys slabs of fro-

▼ *A children's zoo includes animals that children may safely feed.*

▲ *Elephants are always a big attraction in any zoo.*

zen horsemeat. Truckloads of hay arrive for grazing and browsing animals. Fruits and vegetables, as well as insects, mealworms, or other worms are needed for many small mammals and birds. Big zoos have *commissaries*, or food centers. The commissary staff manufacture special diet cakes and pellets, which are convenient for feeding many animals. These cakes are mixtures of nourishing foods that supply protein, carbohydrates, fats, minerals, and vitamins.

Obtaining Animals for a Zoo Some zoo animals are purchased from professional *animal dealers*. The dealers often buy the animals from hunters or trappers, who specialize in capturing wild animals. Many countries now prohibit the trade in wild animals, especially of endangered species.

Many zoo animals are born in captivity. An important part of a zoo's work is to find ways to breed animals that are scarce. New populations, born in zoos, could save some rare animals from becoming extinct. Zoo directors from different countries have organized the Wild Animal Propagation Trust. It works to get zoos to cooperate in building populations of rare animals.

Zoos obtain animals in other ways, too. Sometimes people, or governments, give animals as gifts. Zoos also trade animals with each other. Zoos all around the world keep in close touch and exchange their knowledge.

■ LEARN BY DOING

You can learn a great deal by visiting a zoo, and you'll have fun while you are learning. But make sure that you obey the zoo rules, because they were made to protect you and the animals. When zoo officials put up signs that tell you not to feed a certain animal, it is because the food you might have with you would be bad for it. ■

ALSO READ: ANIMAL, ZOOLOGY.

ZOOLOGY Zoology is the study of animals. Zoologists collect facts on how different animals are structured, how they function, and how they grow. Some zoologists work in laboratories doing careful experiments. Others work out-of-doors, studying animals in their natural surroundings. Modern zoology is such a large subject that most zoologists study just one special branch, or separate science, in the field. For instance, a zoologist might be an expert in *ecology*, the study of how animals relate to their surroundings and to each other. Some zoologists concentrate on particular functions or body parts found in all animals. Other zoologists study particular animals or groups of animals.

Anatomy is the study of the body parts and structure of animals. *Physiology* is the study of life processes, such as digestion and reproduction. *Cytology* is the study of cells—the "building blocks" of which all animal bodies are made. The science of *genetics* shows how characteristics of parents are passed along to their young. *Taxonomy* is the science or technique of placing, or *classifying*, animals into

▲ *Zoology, the study of animals, helps us understand the delicate balances of nature and how to protect endangered species such as the panda. Through zoology we know that pandas rely mainly on bamboo shoots for their food. So preservation of bamboo forests is essential.*

ZOOLOGY

▲ *It was through studies of the rhesus monkey that zoologists discovered much about human blood systems and disorders. Some people have what is called the Rhesus factor, and their blood is said to be Rhesus positive or negative—or Rh+ or Rh–.*

groups according to their relationships with each other.

A *vertebrate zoologist* specializes in animals with backbones, such as human beings, cats, dogs, or fishes. The *invertebrate zoologist* explores the world of animals without backbones, such as insects, mollusks, and worms. *Ornithologists* study birds, *herpetologists* study snakes, *icthyologists* study fish, and *entomologists* study insects. Zoology overlaps many other sciences. Together with *botany*, the study of plants, it forms *biology*, the study of all living things. Zoologists use *chemistry* to study the chemical properties of animals, and *physics* to study the effects of different forces on animals.

Zoology is important to people in many ways. Understanding the way animals function helps scientists to learn how human beings function. For example, new understanding of the way heartbeats are controlled came from studies of horseshoe crabs. Zoological science is applied in the conservation of wildlife resources, as well as in agriculture. Without zoology, it would be impossible to save many endangered wild animals.

History of Zoology Early people had to know a lot about animals. Wild animals were hunted for food, so hunters studied animals and their habits. Later, animals like cows, sheep, and dogs were kept as domestic animals. Farmers learned what they could about their animals to keep them healthy.

In the 300's B.C., the Greek philosopher Aristotle made careful studies of animal life. He dissected many animals and made careful notes on what he saw. Aristotle's work, with its mistakes, was considered the basis of zoological knowledge for the next 1500 years. There were few advances in zoology during this time. Then from the 1200's onward, people began to travel to distant places and discovered many strange, new ani-

mals, then unknown. Advances in anatomy began to be made in the 1300's.

In the 1500's, the Flemish surgeon Andreas Vesalius dissected human cadavers and corrected mistakes made by Aristotle. In 1660, the Italian anatomist Marcello Malpighi used a microscope and discovered capillaries, the tiny blood vessels that connect arteries and veins.

The microscope was an important tool in the growth of zoology. Using it, Anton van Leeuwenhoek discovered bacteria and protozoans, and Robert Hooke studied and described the cell.

Until the 1750's, animals and plants were known only by their popular names and descriptions. This caused great confusion. Then the Swedish botanist Carolus Linnaeus developed a system in which each separate kind of plant and animal was given a two-word Latin name. For example, *Panthera leo* is the scientific name for lion. Linnaeus's system made zoological study more effective and still serves as the basis for classifying living things.

In the 1800's, more zoologists began to study the strange animal life in exotic lands. This led to one of the most important ideas in science, Charles Darwin's theory of the origin of the species. According to Darwin's

▼ *Charles Darwin, whose ideas did much to shape the modern science of zoology.*

theory, different species (kinds) arise as a result of the "survival of the fittest." Animals that are better suited to their surroundings are more likely to survive. Individual variations that make an animal more fit are also those most likely to be passed on to future generations.

In this century, great advances have been made in zoology. Much has been learned about the chemistry of life and how characteristics are passed from parents to offspring. The behavior of animals is being studied. Ecology has achieved a new importance as people have realized that the resources for life on Earth are limited.

Zoology as a Career Zoology can be a fascinating career for someone who is interested in animals. If you should decide to become a zoologist, you will eventually study zoology in college. In the meantime, you should learn all you can about animals.

■ LEARN BY DOING

Observe how animals live. Why are birds quick and lively, while turtles are slow? Why do dogs eat meat, while rabbits eat plants? You can see many different animals at a zoo, but you can also find many animals just by turning over a rock or digging in the ground. Worms and insects can be as informative as larger animals. ■

ALSO READ: AGASSIZ, LOUIS; AGRICULTURE; AMPHIBIAN; ANATOMY; ANIMAL; ANIMAL KINGDOM; ARISTOTLE; BACTERIA; BIOCHEMISTRY; BIOLOGY; BIRD; BOTANY; COELENTERATE; CONSERVATION; CRUSTACEAN; DARWIN, CHARLES; ECHINODERM; ECOLOGY; EVOLUTION; FISH; FOOD WEB; GENETICS; INSECT; LIFE; LINNAEUS, CAROLUS; MAMMAL; MARINE LIFE; MEDICINE; MICROSCOPE; MOLLUSK; NATURE STUDY; PROTIST; RARE ANIMAL; REPTILE; RODENT; SCIENCE; VERTEBRATE; VETERINARY MEDICINE; ZOO.

SOME BRANCHES OF ZOOLOGY

Anatomy   The study of the way living things are made

Botany   The study of plants

Ecology   The study of how living things relate to their environments

Embryology   The study of how animals grow and develop

Entomology   The study of insects

Histology and **Cytology**   The study of the structure of body cells making up organs (histology) and tissues (cytology)

Ornithology   The study of birds

Paleontology   The study of the fossil remains of living things

Pathology   The study of animal diseases

Physiology   The study of how animals' bodies work

Taxonomy   The study of the classification of animals

ZWORYKIN, VLADIMIR KOSMA (1889–1982) Vladimir Zworykin, who was born in Russia, was a pioneer in the development of early television. He studied in France but, when World War I broke out, he went back to Russia to help his country. However, when the Communists took over Russia in 1917, he left for the United States.

In this country he made most of the inventions that led to television. (The Scottish scientist John Logie Baird made similar inventions, but Baird's systems were primitive and have been abandoned.) Zworykin realized that the *cathode-ray tube* could be used to make pictures on a screen coated with fluorescent substances called *phosphors*. The cathode-ray tube gives off a stream of electrons, and these make the phosphors glow whenever they strike them. By 1924, Zworykin had invented what he called a *kinescope*, a type of cathode-ray tube that could be used to make a television picture.

A few years later he invented the *iconoscope*. This was the first practicable television camera, though modern television cameras work in a different way. During the 1930's, he did much to improve the electron microscope.

ALSO READ: CHEMISTRY, MICROSCOPE, TELEVISION.

▲ *Vladimir Zworykin, pioneer of television.*

INDEX

USING THE INDEX

An index is a key to the contents of a book. The index section of the *Young Students Learning Library* is arranged to help you find information quickly and easily. It lists all the articles by name and all the important subjects and people within each one.

HOW THE ENTRIES ARE ARRANGED This may be the first time you have used *alphabetical order*. Your *Learning Library* is arranged in this way. It is an easy way to put articles about so many subjects in an orderly fashion. The same is also true of the index. You will find it easy to use. You just have to know your alphabet. As you look for a subject in the index, think to yourself, 'What letter comes before the one I see here? What letter comes after it?'

The index entries are in alphabetical order, letter-by-letter, even if the entry has more than one word. For example, in the index you can find entries in the following order:

> West Indies
> Westo Indians
> Westphalia
> West Point

The first four letters are the same in those entries—W-e-s-t. In this example it is the fifth letter that will determine which entry goes first alphabetically. You should pay no attention to the space between West and Indies, Westo and Indians, West and Point. Comparing the letters after West you find that 'I' of Indies comes first, the 'o' of Westo, and finally 'p' of Westphalia and West Point. The order of the last two is determined by the 'h' in Westphalia and 'o' in West Point.

Now turn to these entries:

> Stone
> Stone Age
> Stonehenge
> Stone, Lucy
> Stone Mountain

The same principle holds true here; the order after the letters S-t-o-n-e are arranged by the next available letter, ignoring spaces and punctuation.

PAGE NUMBERS Page numbers are given in the form of volume number/page number, thus 18/2195 refers to volume 18 page 2195. If the subject spans more than one page then it is shown as a thru-number 7/776–7. This indicates that the subject is in volume 7 and on pages 776 and 777. Page numbers given in **boldface type** (heavy and dark) indicate where the main reference to the subject is to be found. Thus in the entry:

> **Frogs**, 2/130–1, 9/**1013–14**, 10/1183, 13/1570

the main reference with the maximum amount of information will be found in volume 9 pages 1013 to 1014, but there will also be found other references in less detail on the other pages. You should always check the boldface entries first and then the others if you need more information.

Page numbers in *italic type* (slanting) refer to pages on which will be found illustrations. Thus

Frost fairs, 9/*1015*

refers to an illustration of a frost
fair in volume 9 page 1015. If you
are only looking for pictures of a
subject or a person you can ignore
the page numbers in ordinary type
and just look for those in italic.

Page numbers that have an
asterisk * attached to them indicate
that the article on this page
contains a *Learn by Doing* project.

MAIN ENTRIES The main
entries are divided into two types.
Those that are in **boldface** type
(dark and heavy) refer to the main
headings of the articles as they
appear in this *Learning Library*.
Entries in ordinary type refer to
the subjects and people which are
found within these main articles.

SUBENTRIES A main heading
may have several subheadings.
There are two main reasons for
these. Firstly they are used to divide
up a large article that covers several
pages into its main topics. So if you
look up the entry for 'Libraries' you
will see that it has been broken
down to 'bookmobiles', 'catalogs',
'classification' and so on.
Secondly, subentries are used to
bring together subjects which are
scattered throughout the book.
Thus under 'Human body' you
will not only find the page
numbers referring to the main
article, but subheadings of all the
other articles throughout the *Young
Students Learning Library* dealing
with aspects of the body. For
example:

Human body, 10/1224–5,
10/*1224*
    aging, 1/50
    anatomy, 2/133
    antibodies, 2/177
    biochemistry, 3/*340*
    blood, 3/359–60
    bone, 3/366, 3/*366*
    brain, 4/382–4, 4/*383*
    breathing, 4/387–9, 4/*388*

Aa

Ee

(continued)

Ff

Gg

Ii

(continued)

Jj

Ll

Oo

Pp

Ss

Syracuse, Damocles, 6/695
Syracuse (N.Y.), 4/446
Syracuse (Sicily), 4/*490*, 8/*881*
Syr Darya, 2/195
Syria, 13/1589, 20/**2372–3**, 20/*2372–3*

Tt

Tabby cats, 4/488
Table tennis, 20/**2374–5**, 20/*2375*
Tachina flies, 8/967
Tack, horse riding, 10/1207–8
Tacks, sailing, 18/2153, 18/*2153*
Taconic Mountains, 21/2518
Taconite, 11/1302
Tactical Air Command (TAC), 1/63
Tadpoles, 2/130, 2/131, 2/*152*,
    9/1013, 9/*1013*, 13/1570. 14/1721
Tadzhik, 19/2282
Taft, Robert Alphonso, 20/2375
Taft, Robert Alphonso Jr., 20/2375
Taft, William Howard, 16/1914,
    16/*1968*, 18/2136, 19/*2355*,
    20/**2375–6**, 20/*2375*
Tagalog, 16/1914
Tagus River, 16/1982
Tahiti, 6/653
    Gauguin, Paul, 9/1047
Taiga, 2/150, 19/2282
Tailors, 5/580
Tails, monkeys, 14/1635
Taipa, 12/1472
T'ai Tsung, 5/538
Taiwan, 5/540, 13/1508, 20/**2376–7**,
    20/*2376*
    Chiang Kai–shek, 5/**525–6**
    Sun Yat–sen, 19/2354
Taj Mahal, 11/*1247*, 11/1254,
    20/**2377**, 20/*2377*
Tajumulco, 10/1123
Takahe, 8/*954*
Talc, 13/*1597*
Tallahatchie River, 13/1610
Talleyrand, 1/30
Tallinn, 7/869
Tallow, 8/917
Tallow candles, 4/456
Tall tales, 8/972
Tallulah Gorge, 1/25
Talmud, 11/1344, 11/1345
Tamanduа, 2/172
Tamayo, Rufino, 15/1861, 15/1862,
    15/*1862*, 15/1863
Tamerlane, 11/1254
Tamils, 19/2323
Tampico, 13/1573
Tana, Lake, 15/1776
Tanganyika, 20/2378
Tanganyika, Lake, 1/43, 20/2378
Tang Dynasty, 16/1988
Tangerines, 5/555
Tangier, 14/1648
Tanglewood, 13/1528
Tanguy, Eves, *At Four O'Clock in
    Spring, the Hope*, 19/*2359*,
    19/2360
Tank cars, 17/2054
Tankers, 13/1564
    ships, 18/2206
    trucks, 20/2469, 20/*2470*
Tanks, aquarium, 2/186–90
Tanks, military, 20/**2377–8**, 20/*2377*

Tanning, 12/1408
Tanzania, 20/**2378–9**, 20/*2378*
Taoism, 2/243, 17/2079, 20/**2379**
Taos, 4/476
Tape recordings, 17/2072, 17/*2072*
    cassettes, 4/482
Tapestry, 20/**2379–80**, 20/*2380*
    history, 20/2380
Tapeworm, 16/1876
Tapirs, 20/**2380–1**, 20/*2381*
Taproots, 16/1939
Tara, 11/1301
Tarantella, 8/970
Target shooting, 18/2214, 18/*2214*
Tariffs, 5/574, 11/1292, 20/2382,
    20/2445
Tarkington, Booth, 11/1255
Tarnishing, 6/661
Tarquinius Superbus, 18/2129
Tartans, 18/2176
Tartars, 18/2145
Tarzan, 4/417, 4/*417*
Tasman, Abel, 3/265
Tasmania, 3/265
Tasmanian wolves, 3/268, 17/*2064*,
    17/2065
Taste, 20/**2381**★, 20/*2381*
Tattoos, 18/2233
Taxco, 13/1573, 15/*1784*
Tax Court, 6/667
Taxes, 20/**2381–2**, 20/*2382*
Taxonomists, 3/342
Taxonomy, plant, 3/375
Taylor, Claudia, 11/1339
Taylor, Elizabeth, 1/27
Taylor, Richard, 20/2382
Taylor, Sarah, 6/701, 20/2382
Taylor, Zachary, 6/701, 8/928,
    13/*1572*, 20/**2382–3**, 20/*2383*
Tbilisi, 19/*2284*
Tchaikovsky, Peter Ilyich, 17/2041,
    20/**2383–4**, 20/*2383*
Tea, 2/*244*, 11/*1252*, 20/**2384–5**,
    20/*2384*
Teach, Edward (Blackbeard),
    16/1935, 16/*1935*
Teaching, 20/**2385–6**, 20/*2385*
Teal, 7/771
Teale, Edwin Way, 19/2318
Technology:
    aerospace, 1/40
    agriculture, 1/55–6
    inventions, 11/1292–5, 11/*1292–5*
    patents, 16/1884–5
Tecumseh, 10/1155–6, 11/1256,
    20/**2386**, 20/*2386*, 21/2541
Teenagers, adolescence, 1/34–5
Tees, 9/1091
Teeth, 20/**2386–8**, 20/*2386–7*
    care of, 20/2387–8
    chewing, 6/730
    dentistry, 6/717–18, 6/*716–18*
    fillings, 9/1090
    kinds of, 20/2386–7
    milk teeth, 20/2387
    rodents, 18/2115
    snails, 19/2243
    structure, 20/2387
Tektite II, 15/1821
Tel Aviv, 11/1309
Telecommunications, 20/**2388**,
    20/*2388*
    Morse Code, 14/1651
Teleconferencing, 20/2392

Telegraph, 5/611, 20/**2388–90**,
    20/*2389*
    Marconi, Guglielmo, 13/1513–14
    Morse, Samuel F.B., 14/1650
Telepathy, 8/897
Telephones, 1/*117*, 5/611, 5/*612*,
    7/801, 7/*817*, 20/2388, 20/*2388*,
    20/**2390–3**★, 20/*2390–2*
    Bell, Alexander Graham, 3/329
    communication satellites, 5/612,
    5/614
    modems, 5/624
    special services, 20/2392–3
Teleprinters, 20/2388, 20/2389
Telescopes, 2/250, 2/*250*, 12/1416,
    15/1763, 15/*1763*, 20/**2393–5**★,
    20/*2393–4*
    observatories, 15/1813–14,
    15/*1813–14*
    radio astronomy, 17/2050–1,
    17/*2050–1*
    radio telescopes, 2/251
Teletype, 14/1651
Television, 20/2388, 20/**2395–8**,
    20/*2395–7*
    acting, 1/28
    Baird, John Logie, 3/291–2
    broadcasting, 20/**2398–2400**,
    20/*2398–2400*
    cameras, 4/*442*, 7/825
    color, 20/2396–7
    commercials, 1/38
    communication satellites, 5/612–13
    control rooms, 20/2399
    effect on motion pictures, 14/1663
    journalism, 11/1342–3
    makeup, 12/1488
    news broadcasts, 20/2399
    receivers, 7/*825*
    video, 21/2524–5
    videotape rooms, 20/2399
    Zworykin, Vladimir Kosma,
    22/2649
Tell, William, 12/*1411*, 20/**2400**,
    20/*2400*
Telstar spacecraft, 19/2288
Tema, 9/1074
Temminck's cat, 4/490
Temne, 18/2218
Tempera, 15/1860
Temperate grasslands, animal life,
    2/150
Temperate marine climate, 5/576
Temperate zones, 21/2562
Temperature:
    cold, 10/1168–70
    cryogenics, 6/682
    fever, 8/926
    heat, 10/1168–70
    thermometers, 20/2422
Temperature scale, 20/**2400–1**,
    20/*2401*
    conversion table, 20/2401
Temple of Neptune, 2/*201*
Temples, 20/**2402**, 20/*2402*
    pagodas, 15/1857, 15/*1857*
    Roman, 18/2119
Temple, Shirley, 1/*28*, 7/750,
    14/1663
Tena, Lake, 7/871
Ten Commandments, 6/673, 11/1344,
    12/1399
Tendons, 14/1676
Tendrils, 12/1404

Tenerife, 4/454
Teng Hsiao–p'ing, 5/540, 13/1508,
    20/**2402–3**, 20/*2403*
Tengmalm's owl, 15/*1852*
Tennessee, 20/**2403–5**, 20/*2404–5*
    climate, 20/2404
    employment, 20/2404
    history, 20/2404
    land, 20/2403–4
    map, 20/*2405*
    state emblems, 20/*2405*
Tennessee Hills, 13/1612
Tennessee River, 6/694, 20/2403
Tennessee-Tombigbee Waterway,
    4/454
Tennessee Valley Authority (TVA),
    6/694, 17/2024, 17/*2024*,
    18/2134, 19/2249, 20/2403,
    21/2490
Tennessee walking horses, 10/1206
Tenniel, Sir John, 5/533, 12/*1447*
Tennis, 20/**2406–7**, 20/*2406–7*
    Gibson, Althea, 9/1076–7, 9/*1077*
Tennyson, Alfred, 6/675, 20/**2407**,
    20/*2407*
Tenochtitlán, 3/284, 6/662, 11/1267,
    13/1575
Tenors, 18/2227
Ten pin bowling, 4/378–9, 4/*379*
Tentacles, 15/1822, 15/*1822*
Tenth Amendment, 3/340
Tents, 18/2204, 20/**2408**, 20/*2408*
Tenzing Norkay, 8/*892*, 8/893,
    10/1185, 14/1672
Teotihuacán, 11/1259, 17/2034
Teresa, Mother, 15/1779,
    20/**2408–9**, 20/*2409*
Tereshkova, Valentina, 2/*248*
Termites, 1/*11*, 11/*1279*, 20/**2409**,
    20/*2409*
Terns, 10/1129, 10/*1129*, 18/*2181*,
    18/2182
Terpsichore, 14/1678
Terrain, climate and, 5/576
Terramycin, 7/768
Terra Nova, 14/1713
Terrapins, 20/2478
Terrariums, 20/**2410**★, 20/*2410*
Terrell, Mary Church, 5/563
Terriers, 6/747
Terrorism, 20/**2411**, 20/*2411*
Tesserae, mosaics, 14/1651–2
Testa, 18/2187
Testes, 9/*1081*
Testimonies, court system, 6/666
Test matches, 6/672
Testosterone, 10/1201
Tests, psychological, 17/2019
Teton Indians, 18/2228
Teton Mountains, 22/*2626*
Tetracycline, 2/177
Tetzel, Johann, 12/1470
Tewkesbury, battle of, 21/2543
Texas, 1/*117*, 16/1969, 20/**2411–15**,
    20/*2411–14*
    Alamo, 1/84–5
    climate, 20/2412
    Dallas, 6/693
    employment, 20/2414
    history, 20/2412–14
    land, 20/2411–12
    map, 20/*2413*
    state emblems, 20/*2413*
Textbooks, 3/368

Ww

Xx

Yy

Zz